THE SECRETS OF

CHINESE
ASTROLOGY

THE SECRETS OF
CHINESE
ASTROLOGY

DEREK WALTERS

GRAMERCY BOOKS
NEW YORK

This 2005 edition is published by Gramercy Books, an imprint of Random House Value Publishing, a division of Random House, Inc., New York, by arrangement with Octopus Publishing Group Ltd.

Gramercy is a registered trademark and the colophon is a trademark of Random House, Inc.

Random House

New York • Toronto • London • Sydney • Auckland

www.randomhouse.com

Printed and bound in China

A catalog record for this title is available from the Library of Congress.

ISBN 0-517-22702-9

10 9 8 7 6 5 4 3 2 1

CONTENTS

INTRODUCTION

This book was compiled with three aims. The first is to introduce the newcomer to this fascinating subject easily and comfortably. The second is to give readers who are already familiar with the subject some suggestions and guidance on the interpretation of Chinese horoscopes. The third is to navigate the murky waters that lie between the simple everyday Animal Signs and the technical intricacies of more advanced Chinese astrology.

Some of the 'secrets' of Chinese astrology revealed here show how in most cases the complex business of compiling a horoscope chart can be streamlined without compromising either validity or accuracy. Other 'secrets' give the historical background behind some technical aspects encountered in more advanced Chinese astrology. Most of the secrets, however, are concerned with the interpretation of the horoscope.

The material presented in this book deals almost exclusively with the role of the 12 Animals of the Chinese Zodiac, but this is not just a popular guide to 'star signs'. The technical term for the familiar 12 Animals is the 12 Branches, and although the Chinese Animal Zodiac is a comparatively recent innovation in Chinese astrology, the 12 Branches on which they are based go right back to the dawn of writing.

THE ROLE OF THE 12 ANIMALS

The invention of the 12 Animals, probably by Buddhist monks in Central Asia, was a masterstroke, for the way that they help in the understanding of a Chinese horoscope cannot be bettered. The names of the 12 Animals were selected with meticulous care. Not only does each one relate significantly to a particular time of day and season of the year, its natural characteristics relate to the astrological interpretation of the ancient Chinese signs. With the 12 Animals, mystic oriental algebra is replaced with a symbolism that is immediately comprehensible. Indeed, so carefully were the animal names chosen that even the relationships between the various signs, whether fortunate or unfavourable, can easily be identified.

CONSTRUCTING A HOROSCOPE

In the past, the most awesome aspect of Chinese astrology was getting to grips with the complexities of the Chinese calendar, yet the plain fact is that in at least four out of five cases a Chinese horoscope of professional quality can be constructed for someone without any recourse to a Chinese calendar at all. A few straightforward tables and a little arithmetic is all that you need. For the remaining 20 per cent, nearly all of them can be dealt with in just one or two extra steps, but of course there will always be borderline cases that require more detailed scrutiny.

Although this book is primarily concerned with the 12 Animals (or Branches), occasional references to other aspects of the Chinese horoscope (such as the 'stems and branches' or the philosophy of the Five Elements) that are unique to Chinese astrology are inevitable. As far as is practicable, however, such excursions into the unfamiliar are kept to a minimum, and introduced gently. Occasional remarks concerning the historical development of Chinese astrology will lead to a deeper understanding of the subject.

A QUESTION OF TIME

Because the main purpose of the book is to present an introductory picture of Chinese astrology, the reader is not going to be detained with such precise details as whether daylight saving time was in force in Buenos Aires in 1946, or what allowances should be made for time zone changes on the Lithuanian border, or the exact moment when the Sun reaches its highest point over Canberra. For those who wish to enter such labyrinths, there are several computer programmes on the market that will unravel these technical matters. The main thing is to become familiar with the essential process of setting up and interpreting a horoscope, and this is best achieved by practising with a few straightforward examples that fall within the limits outlined on page 132.

Once you have mastered a few simple guidelines, you will be surprised how easily you will be able to assess the general traits of someone's personality. Practise your new-found skills and astonish people (as well as yourself) with your perceptive insight. But, if you wish to remain popular, choose only the nice things to say about them!

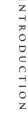

GETTING
STARTED

WHAT IS CHINESE ASTROLOGY?

The Chinese character for the number 3 is made of three lines, one above the other. The top line is said to represent Heaven, the bottom line the Earth, and the middle line the people who live on the Earth, and below Heaven. The number 3 also represents the three kinds of Fate that rule our lives. The Heaven Fate is that which is given to us, over which we have no control. The Earth Fate reveals the place and circumstances in which we live, and over which, to a certain extent, we do have a choice. The Human Fate is what we do with our lives and how the consequences that we have to live with are the result of our actions. Thus, whether we become rich and famous, poor and self-effacing, happy or unhappy, depends only partly on being in the right place (the Earth Fate) at the right time (the Heaven Fate), but also to a great extent on our Human Fate – what we do with the chances offered to us.

SKYWATCHERS

In 212 BCE it was recorded that 300 astronomers were employed at the imperial observatory, watching the heavens day and night. Comets, meteors and other celestial phenomena were carefully described and their significance debated.

THE ORIGINS OF CHINESE ASTROLOGY

From the very earliest times, Chinese soothsayers kept watch over the skies day and night to record any signs that might indicate Heaven's approval or displeasure. Eclipses, comets and other phenomena were carefully recorded and their significance pondered, and when anything untoward occurred, the events were meticulously noted together with the

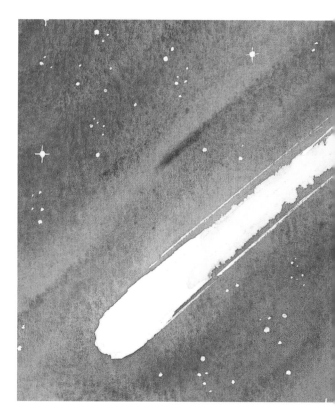

date on fragments of bone. These 'oracle bone' inscriptions are the earliest examples of Chinese writing, the forerunners of the Chinese characters used today. Several centuries later, Buddhist monks who were bringing the Scriptures from India, understandably encumbered by the Chinese signs used for their calendar, devised the cycle of 12 Animals as a way of making the names of the months and the years easier to remember.

As time passed, the philosophy and rich symbolism inherent in Chinese astrology became progressively more dense and complex. By the 18th century it had grown into such a vast subject that the section on astrology in the official Chinese Imperial Encyclopaedia of 1726 ran to an incredible 2,500 chapters.

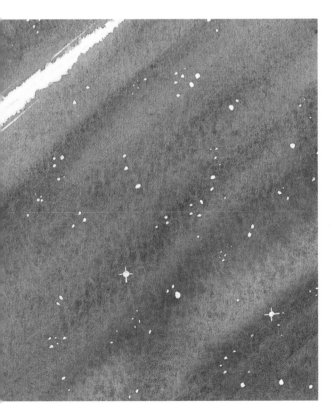

Over the past few hundred years, Chinese practitioners have strived to improve their art, and in doing so have continued to borrow ideas from the Western system of astrology, so that the closer one gets to the present day, the greater the resemblance between later Chinese and Western astrology.

THE 12 ANIMAL SIGNS OF THE CHINESE ZODIAC

The most familiar aspect of Chinese astrology is the 'Zodiac' of the 12 Animals. But there are three curious facts about this so-called Zodiac. Firstly, as far as Chinese history goes, the 12 Animals are a comparatively recent introduction into Chinese astrology; secondly, it is highly unlikely that they are a Chinese concept, and thirdly, apart from the fact that there are 12 signs, the cycle of 12 Animals is nothing like the Western Zodiac.

Exactly when the animal names were introduced into Chinese astrology and by whom remains a mystery. When the official imperial court historian Sima Qian wrote his book on astrology in the 2nd century BCE he never mentioned them, but some eight centuries later, Buddhist monks at a remote retreat in north-west China, hard at work on their manuscripts of astrological predictions, illustrated them with exquisite pen-drawings of the year deities, identifying them by hats, each depicting one of the 12 Animals.

The Venetian explorer Marco Polo, crossing Mongolia in the 13th century, heard about the 12 Animals and recalled having seen a horoscope in China in which various animal

When I first encountered Chinese astrology I thought that its obvious weakness was the way it categorized people by the year in which they were born. Did this condemn all students born in a certain year to fail their examinations, for example? Yet the more I thought about it, the more I realized that this was in fact the great strength of Chinese astrology. Any teacher will tell you that each year's intake of students has its own overall characteristic, which can be ascribed not to any particular individual, but to the group as a whole. And, of course, Chinese astrology does not just look at the year in which a person is born; the month, the day and even the hour have to be considered. From these Four Columns, it is possible to find out about people's strengths and susceptibilities, their ideal partners in life, the kind of employment that would suit them best, and even which times are most favourable for them.

names were given to the year, month, day and hour. He mentioned them in his memoirs, although he garbled the names somewhat and got them in the wrong order.

Again, while Tibetan historical documents have always used the 12 Animals to designate the years, official Chinese calendars, even today, give the animals of the years rather deprecatingly in tiny print, almost as an afterthought. All the evidence suggests that the 12 animal names were imported from Central Asia, through Mongolia and Tibet. This struck home to me some 40 years ago when I was travelling through the mountains in northern Turkey and Iran. I found that illiterate Kurdish shepherds reckoned the years and their ages not by the Western calendar dates, but by the names of the 12 Animals familiar to me as the 'Chinese Zodiac'.

It is fascinating to speculate that the 12 animal names, now so closely associated with the Chinese calendar, may actually be the remnants of an even older shamanic culture from Central Asia or beyond, which was in place long before Buddhism took root.

THE CHINESE AND WESTERN ZODIACS

In Western astronomy (and astrology) the word 'zodiac' refers to a belt of constellations across the sky through which the Sun, Moon and planets appear to travel. The meaning, by extension, also means the times of the year that used to correspond to those divisions. The Chinese Animal Signs, however, are only ever used to describe periods of time, in particular the years. There is only one Animal Sign that may have taken its name from an old Chinese constellation, and that is the Dragon. Significantly, it is the only one of the 12 Animals that is mythological. Some scholars have suggested that the 12 animal names used to be the names of special ritual foods – as apart from beef, lamb and pork, such delicacies as snake, dog and even tiger occasionally appear on Chinese menus. However, dragon meat would be hard to come by.

The fact that all the names in the sequence are animals reveals another substantial difference between the two Zodiacs: in the Western Zodiac, four of the signs are human, and one, Libra, is not even a living creature. In effect, since the word 'zodiac' refers specifically to animals, it is a far more appropriate word to describe the Chinese signs than the Western ones.

THE NORTH-SOUTH DEBATE

The symbolism used to describe the periodic influences in Chinese astrology is often illustrated by references to the four seasons of the northern hemisphere. Naturally, people who live in the southern hemisphere frequently ask if any changes should be made to the calculations to account for the reversal of the seasons. Before this important question is answered, here are a few points to consider.

Ancient Chinese astronomers knew that the Earth was a globe, and that it turned on an axis (the *taiqi*, or *tai chi*). They knew therefore that it had two poles, one in the frozen north, and that consequently, the other must be in a region that was incredibly hot! (In Chinese mythology, the Old Man of the South Pole is always portrayed enveloped in flames.)

CELESTIAL MESSENGERS
Chinese astrologers of ancient times recognized four types of celestial body: the Sun, the Moon, the stars and the planets.

When Chinese philosophers of old were teaching, the progress of the four northerly seasons helped their students to form an understanding of the way in which the rises and falls of fortunes had their parallel in the four seasons of the year. But the use of the seasons was only symbolic. The teachers' listeners would have come from many different parts of China – from the icy wastes of the Himalayas, to the torrid jungles of the rain forests. However, the position of the Earth relative to the universe around it is unchanged: the Great Bear will always be in the northern sky, and the Southern Cross in the South, whether one lives in Washington, District of Columbia, or Wellington, New Zealand.

On a practical note, supposing that allowances were indeed made for the two hemispheres – where exactly would the change start? At the equator, maybe, or somewhere in the tropics, where the Sun is overhead for at least two days in the year? For in the tropics, people spend part of their life in the southern hemisphere, and the remainder in the northern.

Thus, references to the seasons are symbolic, designed for the enlightenment of the average Chinese student living in a northern temperate latitude. The ruling principle of Chinese astrology is the interpretation of the Heaven Fate, revealed by Heaven's messengers, the stars, the Sun, the Moon and the planets. These are the markers of time, which record when fortunes rise and fall, like the ebb and flow of the tide. Just as autumn turns to winter, and winter to spring, so the highs and lows of life are as inevitable

as the changing of the seasons, or the phases of the Moon. The secrets of Chinese astrology belong to the Heaven Fate. What we do with the Heaven Fate is entirely up to us.

STEMS AND BRANCHES

The Chinese have two ways of writing the date; the most usual is similar to our standard calendar where the months are numbered from 1 to 12 and the days from 1 to 30. Another system uses special signs called 'stems and branches'. The stems are a sequence of ten signs, originally the names of a ten-day week; the branches are a sequence of 12 signs, probably adopted from the 12 divisions of the day. Combined, stems and branches make a sequence of 60 pairs of signs. This system has been used for more than four thousand years. During the 1st century, it was decided to apply it as a means of reckoning the years, and then, much later, the sequences were added to the months and hours as well. The four stem-and-branch combinations for the year, month, day, and hour are known as the Four Columns. Because each Column is a pair of signs, they are sometimes called the Eight Characters or, in Chinese, *bazi*. Some time during the 7th or 8th century the names of the 12 Animals were introduced to supplement the 12 branch signs. Branches 1 to 12 became Rat, Ox, Tiger, Rabbit, Dragon, Snake, Horse, Sheep, Monkey, Rooster, Dog, Pig. Today, most Chinese calendars give the branch signs for the year, month and day, together with the animal names. In every horoscope, there will be four Animal Signs, one each for the year, month, day and time.

The Yin and Yang theory of opposites, despite being a concept more than three thousand years old, is actually the principle on which all modern physics is founded.

Everything, whether material or abstract, has an opposite. If it didn't, it wouldn't exist. More than two thousand years ago the philosopher Lao Tse used a cup to illustrate the principle: the material of the cup was Yang, the inside of it Yin. Although there was nothing inside the cup but space, if the space wasn't there it would have no use as a cup.

The terms Yang and Yin originally referred to the sunny and shaded sides of a hill. Because in ancient times men worked in the fields, in the sun, and the women indoors, in the shade, the terms also came to mean male and female. The expression has expanded to mean all kinds of energy: physical, biological and emotional. Yang is outgoing, Yin is receptive. They are equivalent terms to positive and negative, or plus and minus, but without any connotations of good and bad.

When examining a horoscope chart, a Chinese astrologer likes to see a good balance of Yang and Yin in the signs, in the same way that a Chinese doctor identifies various ailments as the result of an imbalance of Yang and Yin.

The term Great Yang is still used in modern Chinese to mean the Sun itself, while the Moon, less commonly, is referred to as the Great Yin. Thus the standard calendar based on the seasons is known as the Yang calendar, while the Chinese calendar based on the Moon is usually called the Yin calendar.

The Five Elements of Chinese natural science, Wood, Fire, Earth, Metal and Water, have names similar to the Four Elements of Greek philosophy, but there is no other connection. The earliest reference to them in Chinese literature speaks of them as the 'five essentials' needed for working and living, but they are also the names of the five planets known to the ancients: Jupiter, Mars, Saturn, Venus and Mercury.

All aspects of existence can be categorized as belonging to one or more of the Elements, from shapes, colours and materials, to physical appearance and emotions. Wood influences health and well-being, women and children, creativity and artistry. The liver, the eyes, the sight and light are helped by the Wood Element, for which the related emotion is anger. Fire influences intelligence, animal husbandry, heat and circulation.

THE CONSTRUCTIVE SEQUENCE

Wood burns, creating Fire, which leaves ash (Earth) behind. From the Earth we get Metal, which when molten flows like Water, which is needed to make vegetation (Wood) grow.

Its related action is laughter. Earth influences the digestion, land and buildings, and is connected with contemplation. Metal influences the lungs and breathing, money and commerce. Its related emotion is grief. Water, the Element of midnight and winter, rules the urinogenital system. Its emotion is fear. In astrology, it is the time factor that reveals which Elements exert their influences at any given moment. In the sequences described below, each Element is said to be the parent of the next. Wood, for example, is the parent of Fire. Two or more Elements that are next to each other in the sequence (for example Earth and Metal) will be in harmony, and will result in satisfaction and productivity. Where there are alternate Elements in the sequence (such as Fire and Metal or Earth and Water) the result will be discord and conflict.

THE DESTRUCTIVE SEQUENCE

Growing plants deprive Earth of its nourishment; Earth pollutes Water, which puts out Fire. Fire in turn melts Metal, from which we make implements to chop down Wood.

THE ANIMAL SIGN
FOR THE YEAR, MONTH, DAY AND HOUR

THE ANIMAL SIGN FOR THE YEAR

When people talk about their Western Zodiac signs – Aries, Sagittarius, Virgo or whatever – they refer to the particular *time* of the year that they were born. When the Chinese speak of their personal Animal Signs, they mean the actual year they were born. It has long been understood in China that the Animal Zodiac is a reliable way to ascertain whether a prospective couple would make a good match, and there are many folklore proverbs that provide traditional wisdom in these matters. Money, breeding and good looks count for very little if the Animal Signs are incompatible. And that is where our problem begins. For while it is an easy matter for most people to reckon their Animal Sign (see the table on page 22), there remains the question of when the Chinese astrological year begins.

THE CHINESE NEW YEAR

The obvious answer would seem to be that it begins with the Chinese New Year Festival. For the past 350 years this has fallen on the second New Moon after the shortest day, some time between the middle of January and the middle of February (see the table on pages 138–9). This rule will hold fast until 2033, when the New Year Festival will be celebrated on the third New Moon after the shortest day. The expression used is New Year Festival, not New Year's Day, for the date of the start of the Chinese year is a contentious subject for the different schools of Chinese astrology.

In effect, there are as many as five possible choices. The first contender is the date of the Chinese New Year Festival, based on the phases of the Moon. Most ordinary Chinese people would agree that this was practically self-evident. But their astrologers generally opt for a date based on the solar year. The Li Chun, the Beginning of Spring, is the half-way point between the Winter Solstice (the shortest day, about 21 December) and the Spring Equinox (about 21 March). At present, the Beginning of Spring usually falls on 4 February, but the date gradually gets earlier by about a day every 70 years or so. At the beginning of the 20th century it was more often 5 February; by the end of the 21st century it will have advanced to 3 February (see the table on pages 138–9).

Since most Chinese astrologers divide the year into solar rather than lunar months, it makes greater sense to start the year with a date related to the solar calendar.

But a third school of thought maintains that the astrological year begins at the moment the days begin to lengthen; when Yin transforms to Yang; at the moment of the

Winter Solstice itself, between 20 and 22 December. It gets so complicated that some less scrupulous fortune-tellers prefer to use the Western calendar instead.

For most people it does not matter when the Chinese New Year begins, since for anyone whose date of birth is later than 22 February, all five calendars are in agreement.

So for the remaining 15 per cent of people whose birthdays fall before 21 February, what date should be used for the start of the Chinese astrological year?

Most Chinese astrologers I have met agree that the data to be used should be based on the vernal calendar, which begins with the Beginning of Spring in early February. Horoscopes compiled in the 14th, 17th and 19th centuries confirm that this has been the normal practice for many generations.

So here is the general rule. Although some people born in the cross-over period will have assumed that the Animal Sign for their birth year is based on the date of the Chinese New Year Festival, when compiling a horoscope, 4 or 5 February (as shown in the table on pages 138–9) should be used for the start of the Chinese astrological year.

The dates of the Chinese New Year follow a 19-year pattern called the Metonic Cycle. You can see that the Chinese New Year is nearly always the same date 19 years before or later.

Now here is a useful tip. For every year from 1981 until 2016 the astrological year begins on 4 February. Although the date is the same, the actual time creeps forward, so that in 2017 it falls for the first time on 3 February.

Although the Western calendar has been in general use for close on a hundred years in China, older Chinese people still reckon their age not from their date of birth, but from the day of the New Year Festival after they were born. This makes it difficult for passport inspectors and the like to identify a Chinese person from the birthdate, since everyone born in 1940, for example, would give their date of birth as 8 February, the date of the New Year Festival that year.

CHINESE NEW YEAR
As on all important occasions in China, the New Year is celebrated with Dragon Dances. These may have extremely complex choreography, needing several weeks of rehearsal.

TO FIND THE ANIMAL SIGN FOR THE YEAR

Use the table below to find the Animal Sign of the YEAR for anyone whose birthday is after 21 February (for those with birthdays before this date see the table on pages 138–9).

Now turn to the page listed in the BIRTH SIGN column of the table to see what is revealed by the person's year sign.

To discover the person's prospects for any particular year, consult the table below again to see which Animal rules over that year.

Now turn to the page listed in the PROSPECTS column of the table to see whether the year will be favourable or unfavourable.

To see whether two people (provided that both their birthdays fall after 21 February) are destined to be compatible, use the table to find their Animal Signs.

Again, use the page references in the PROSPECTS column of the table to see how the two Animal Signs relate to each other.

ANIMAL SIGN FOR THE YEAR

BIRTH YEAR *(for birthdays after 21 February in any year)*								ANIMAL	BIRTH SIGN *see page*	FOR PROSPECTS *see pages*
1924	1936	1948	1960	1972	1984	1996	2008	Rat	24	86–7
1925	1937	1949	1961	1973	1985	1997	2009	Ox	26	88–9
1926	1938	1950	1962	1974	1986	1998	2010	Tiger	28	90–1
1927	1939	1951	1963	1975	1987	1999	2011	Rabbit	30	92–3
1928	1940	1952	1964	1976	1988	2000	2012	Dragon	32	94–5
1929	1941	1953	1965	1977	1989	2001	2013	Snake	34	96–7
1930	1942	1954	1966	1978	1990	2002	2014	Horse	36	98–9
1931	1943	1955	1967	1979	1991	2003	2015	Sheep	38	100–1
1932	1944	1956	1968	1980	1992	2004	2016	Monkey	40	102–3
1933	1945	1957	1969	1981	1993	2005	2017	Rooster	42	104–5
1934	1946	1958	1970	1982	1994	2006	2018	Dog	44	106–7
1935	1947	1959	1971	1983	1995	2007	2019	Pig	46	108–9

CHART OF THE 12 ANIMALS

This chart tells you at a glance which Animal Signs are favourable together, and which may produce conflict.

Most favourable are those separated by two Animal Signs; most troublesome are those opposite each other.

SIGNS AND SYMBOLS

It is a good idea to learn the names of the 12 Animal Signs in sequence, and to fix the pattern in your head. The animal names were invented to describe the qualities of the signs, not the other way round. For example, the last sign indicated completion and satisfaction, so the Pig was chosen as the symbol of homely contentment. No signs are good or bad; each has both its constructive and less praiseworthy qualities. People who are disappointed that they are not Tigers or Dragons can be thankful that they are not regarded as aggressive or extrovert, while Pigs can take comfort in the fact that such people are regarded as the kindest of the 12 types.

THE RAT

THE RAT, as the first of the Chinese Zodiac signs, signifies a beginning. In the Chinese calendar, the month ruled by the sign of the Rat is the one that includes the shortest day, and on old Chinese and Japanese clocks midnight is depicted by the Rat – signifying the start of a new day. The Rat 'hour' or, more technically, double-hour lasts from 11.00 pm until 1.00 am.

Long before the animal names were invented, the original Chinese character for this first sign also meant a baby, representing the birth of a new period of time. It stands at the point when the Greatest Yin begins to give way to the Yang force, and so signifies creation, inspiration and the generation of ideas or activities.

Because the Rat hour is midnight, it suggests a thinker poring over difficult books late into the night. Given a complex problem or enigma, the Rat will work away into the small hours until the solution is found. While the Rat is good at unravelling complex projects on paper, it shies away from the practical aspects, often leaving others to bring the concepts to fruition. These helpful souls, however, are unlikely to be other Rats, since all Rat people like to be in at the beginning rather than the end. As such they are sociable and mutually supportive, can be wonderfully encouraging and have the contacts to make things happen.

A wry sense of humour means that Rats are sometimes taken too literally and misunderstood, and many a valuable argument is lost through the Rat not putting its point of view in a concise and comprehensible way. But, curiously, they are equally guilty of failing to detect irony when it is used by others.

Rat people tend to be erratic where the household budget is concerned. Certainly they are able to handle it astutely, but their naturally creative nature sometimes allows an inspirational turn of mind to overrule common sense. From time to time the Rat's finances will lurch through some precarious straits, but eventually a safe haven will be reached. It will be a long time before the Rat learns that lean years often follow years of plenty, and that it is wisest to ensure that there is always a store of resources.

Family ties are important for the Rat, but not paramount. Being of independent mind,

The Rat's ideal partner would be either the Dragon or the Monkey, both of whom share the Rat's appreciation of the novel and exotic. Other Rats can be supportive at home, in the workplace or in social life, but because their interests are so similar they are unable to add an extra dimension to the Rat's experience. If the Rat is willing to take a secondary role in a relationship (although this is unlikely) then either the Dog or the Tiger might prove an amenable and stimulating companion.

the Rat is the one member of the family who is likely to set up home away from established roots. In a domestic crisis the Rat's opinions will carry most weight.

Rats are able to follow any career or profession that allows them to use their creative skills. They are good at dealing with people, and with their convincing and possibly manipulative manner they are equally adept at being teachers or counsellors. Since they crave freedom of movement and flexibility of working hours, when they are given positions where they are free to set their own schedules they will work assiduously and give far more of their time to the task than if they were obliged to work within specified limits.

Although unconcerned about their appearance, believing that others should be able to perceive the real person underneath the surface, Rats rise to the occasion and make a good impression.

THE OX

In ancient China, on a day approved by his astrologers, the emperor himself would lead an ox to plough the first furrow of the year. The annual Chinese almanac always begins with a picture of a boy or man standing beside the spring ox, and this association may account for the choice of the ox to represent the close of winter. But since the Ox is the only sign that corresponds to a Western Zodiac sign, Taurus the Bull, it is possible that Chinese astrologers borrowed the symbolism from the West.

People born in Ox years are developers and perfectors, the ones with the foresight and patience to plant an acorn and nurture it until it grows into an oak. They are not afraid of routine activity, and prefer the trusted and established to the novel and uncertain. Their solidly responsible qualities win many admirers in a turbulent world, and thus they can rise to high positions of management and political office. By being resolute in difficult situations and unlikely to swerve from a dedicated direction, they can effortlessly take on the most antagonistic opponents. Of course, their intransigence is likely to win them enemies too, but these are unlikely to be successful in any contest of power. As the Chinese proverb puts it, 'One Ox can fight two Tigers'. Danger is likely to come from the most unexpected source; a friend neglected through an oversight may

take offence at some imagined affront, and prove treacherous.

The Ox belongs to a trio (the others are the Rooster and the Snake) who, in combination, are shrewd financiers and investors. Without the other two, however, the Ox prefers saving to investment.

The Ox naturally gravitates to any professional work connected with the land. Real estate, more particularly the land on which buildings stand, farming land, mining and large-scale engineering works, roads and bridges, are all career areas for the Ox. The Ox would be a valuable asset to any organization, for by its careful and systematic management, the company's finances will improve steadily.

Though the Ox may give the impression of being staid and formal, there is at heart a traditionally romantic streak which will be

The Ox is likely to find a partner close to its working environment, but in an entirely different department. It might be the Rooster from the world of commerce, or the Snake from the legal profession. Despite their opposite outlooks, the Ox and the Rooster are magnetically attracted and a strong link is welded between them; the Ox attracted to the Rooster's looks and bearing, and the Rooster to the honest unpretentiousness of the Ox. Similarly, the match of intellectual and physical qualities in the Ox and Snake makes these a perfect couple, too.

disclosed only to the most intimate circle of friends. The Ox's love of the finer things in literature and the arts will be discreetly hidden, and the occasional revealing flashes of an inner culture will often astonish people who thought they knew every side of the Ox person's character.

In family matters the Ox is likely to try to impose an adherence to old-fashioned values on family members who would prefer to throw off the heavy shackles of domestic restraint. An understanding of both sides of the argument would be beneficial.

The Ox will make a show of not being particularly interested in making a fashion statement, but will always be appropriately dressed for the occasion, choosing a classic line that could not possibly be faulted.

THE TIGER

ACROSS ITS FOREHEAD the Tiger bears the Chinese word for king – wang – proving beyond any possible doubt that the Tiger is the king of the animals. So when ancient Chinese astrologers were searching for a suitable animal for the important first month of the Chinese year, the royal tiger was the obvious choice to lead the calendar.

Kingship symbolizes luxury and dominion, and Tiger people exude confidence, resolutely refusing to accept the possibility that they could be inferior to anyone else. Of course, they are well aware that whatever their misgivings and reluctance, it is their life's duty to take on the responsibilities of leadership, and in this role they are determined to fulfil their obligations. Whatever it takes to get to a position of authority – hard work, money or influence – the Tiger will strive to achieve this aim. Even the quietest and most retiring of Tiger personalities will see to it that it attains some position of privilege where it can exercise its discretionary judgemental powers, no matter how trivial these might be. But most Tigers will reach for the highest post. In doing so, of course, they can make enemies, and they should remember that success always engenders envy and spite in others. In the rush to get to the top, the Tiger needs to be careful who gets pushed aside.

The Tiger's nemesis is always close by. In the Chinese calendar, the Ox marks the end of the old year, the Tiger the beginning of the new one. The obstacles faced by the Tiger do not come from new challenges, but from the impossibility of changing the old order. The Tiger need not fear new faces, no matter how imposing. Dangers arise when it tries to hack away traditional values and established regimes, symbolized by the entrenched Ox. This is when the Tiger fails to achieve its aims.

As a companion, the Tiger is wonderfully stimulating, and those Tigers who are not drawn to physical sporting activities will exercise their wits in mind games, enjoying humorous but kindly banter in debates or verbal competition. To less privileged people the Tiger is benign and encouraging without being condescending, able to listen sympathetically, offering constructive advice. Tigers like to keep up with the latest news, from international crises to celebrity chatter.

In financial matters, the Tiger succeeds best when it is able to direct other people along the path to fortune. By shrewdly helping others, the Tiger can make spectacular gains.

Home life will be stable and disciplinarian without being harsh and oppressive. The family will be close-knit, with strong loyalties between the siblings, but if the Tiger is the youngest member of the family the child will have a rebellious streak and disappoint the parents.

Many Tigers are drawn to the uniformed professions because of the formality and discipline. Thus Tigers will be found in the ranks and staff of the nursing profession, police, fire service and, of course, the armed forces, all careers that give the continued prospect of upward promotion.

In their dress Tigers will be fastidious, turned out in an expensive but refined and sophisticated fashion.

IDEAL COMPANION

Because the Tiger is such a strongly masculine symbol, Chinese parents of old were loath to let their sons marry girls born in the year of the Tiger. 'Never bring a Tigress into the house', was a common admonishment from parents who feared that a woman with such a strong personality would usurp the prospective husband's authority. But if both partners are Tigers, the problem does not arise. The Tiger shares many qualities with the Dog and the Horse, and a mutual respect will form strong ties in a partnership with either of these signs.

THE RABBIT

THE GENTLE RABBIT is the counterpart to the ferocious Tiger. As contrasting as these signs appear, they are really the opposite sides of the same coin: the Tiger conquers by sheer aggression and vitality, the Rabbit conquers just as assuredly through tact and diplomacy. Here is an important lesson: what cannot be achieved through force may be won by subtlety.

Choosing a Rabbit (or Hare: the word is the same in Chinese) to be the fourth sign of the Chinese Zodiac was an easy decision for the astrologers of old. It represents sunrise, a time when rabbits emerge from their warrens. The Rabbit month always includes the Spring Equinox. Thus the sign of the Rabbit is associated directly with the spring and all its joys, the dawn and all its promises, freshness, resurgence, and renewed hopes for the future.

Rabbits have all the tender caring qualities of those who love children and animals. They are also fond of flowers and herbs, and other horticultural pursuits, but they are rarely drawn to large-scale farm management which is less aesthetically pleasing. Another close affinity between the Rabbit and plant care is found in a celebrated Chinese folk tale. The myth tells of a Rabbit that flew to the Moon where it stays to this day, stirring a cauldron of magical potions to prepare the Elixir of Immortality. When Chinese children see the Full Moon, instead of the Man in the Moon they see a picture of the Rabbit busy at its task. Thus the Rabbit is also associated with the healing arts and the preparation of medicines and remedies. It is drawn to any profession that involves tending the sick and the disadvantaged. Money is less important to it than its social responsibilities.

The Rabbit needs company and develops firm friendships. It is probably the least extrovert of the 12 Animals, and is likely to turn away from confrontation. Yet the Rabbit will be stirred to righteous anger if it senses that harm is being done to someone helpless.

The Rabbit is a well-loved member of the family with a natural inclination to help parents and siblings in whatever way it can. It rarely troubles others with its own problems.

The natural rabbit's brilliant eyesight translates into acute discernment when applied to the zodiacal Rabbit, which has an innate ability to distinguish false from genuine.

The typical Rabbit would prefer to be an early riser, but its inclination to follow an active social life is likely to put a strain on its physical well-being. Similarly, if professional duties involve irregular hours, the Rabbit will find it stressful to comply efficiently.

In dress the Rabbit tends towards natural colours and ethnic designs, preferring to blend in with its surroundings.

IDEAL COMPANION

The Rabbit would make an ideal and compliant companion for just about any member of the Chinese Zodiac. But who would be the perfect partner for the Rabbit? Of course other Rabbits, with their many shared interests, would form strong bonds, while the two signs closer to the Rabbit's fondness for children and family life are the home-loving and comfort-seeking Pig and the Sheep with its unwavering devotion. Since the powerful Tiger is the Yang counterpart to the Rabbit's Yin they would make a remarkable but compatible couple. At all costs, however, the Rabbit should spurn the glamorous Dragon, whose magic would soon wear thin.

THE DRAGON

The Dragon is the only Chinese astrological sign that is not a real animal. According to ancient Chinese astronomers, the eastern quarter of the sky was known as the Dragon, this constellation rising in the sky in late spring, the Dragon month. Its mystical origins mean that the Dragon, and its companion sign the Snake, are associated with the supernatural.

Chinese dragons, unlike their Western counterparts, do not have wings, though they are often depicted flying through the sky. The preferred home of the Chinese dragon, however, is in the water, its lairs revealed by the turbulence of whirlpools and maelstroms.

In China the dragon has been the symbol of imperial authority for millennia. It has always been held as the ultimate symbol of good fortune, with pearls issuing from its mouth and gold coins from its nether regions.

The Dragon personality reveals a truly flamboyant character with a love of the exotic, a highly extrovert personality that tends towards the bizarre, eccentric and often outrageous. The Dragon character will make heads turn in astonishment before a word is uttered. In speech, there are never moments of hesitation – only meaningful pauses. When the Dragon commands, others must obey, not out of fear or servility, but out of stupefaction at the Dragon's sheer effrontery.

The Dragon always manages to display wealth. There is never a shortage of cash, although it may not always be in the Dragon's pocket. Indeed, the greatest danger for the Dragon is the need to make extravagant gestures, and in some amazing ways these unbelievable risks nearly always repay their investor handsomely.

Dragon people have agile minds, and in conversation their quick thinking is both mesmerizing and disconcerting. They attract many friends and admirers, but the most devoted of these are frequently driven to despair by the Dragon's apparent lack of stability and direction. To outsiders, it seems that the Dragon's decisions last only as long as it takes to utter the words. It often seems that the Dragon will change its mind on a whim, but this is usually because it finds it difficult to accommodate the slightest changes to already established plans, which it will abandon wholesale rather than alter, no matter how difficult the consequences may be.

In the family the Dragon will offer controversial views on the issues of the moment. Whether these are taken on board or rejected is of no consequence, as long as the water is thrashed around.

Since the Dragon thrives on adulation, and craves recognition for its skills and schemes, it is ideally suited to any career that places it in the public eye. The theatre is its ideal medium, though Dragons will be drawn to the bright lights wherever they shine. They will also be drawn to work in financial institutions, for the clink of gold and the glitter of jewels are the Dragon's spiritual food.

Always unconventional, the Dragon is never afraid to wear what it deems suitable, no matter if this raises an eyebrow or two.

IDEAL COMPANION

The Dragon's special capabilities will be best understood by the studious Rat or the artful Monkey. But under no circumstances should the Dragon allow itself to become involved with the gentle and imploring Rabbit – 'When the Rabbit appears, All the Dragon's fortunes disappear,' says an old Chinese adage. Other suitable companions for the Dragon would be the Tiger or the Horse, while its companion sign, the Snake, would also be understanding and supportive.

THE SNAKE

THE COMPANION SIGN to the Dragon, the Snake is also a sign of mystical prowess, but in a far more restrained way. Where the Dragon is the conjuror, summoning demons from the vast deep, the Snake is more inclined to attain spiritual contact through the process of meditation. According to the Chinese calendar, the Snake month is the first month of summer.

This is when snakes make their first appearance to bask in the mild sunshine. Should they appear at the wrong time, however, they are said to forewarn of impending earthquakes, possibly because, in their dwellings in the ground, they are able to detect the onset of tremors. Snake years are often marked by a series of earthquakes, sometimes devastatingly so.

Just as the Dragon is associated with gold and jade, the Snake is said to be the guardian of buried treasure; perhaps because in digging a hole to hide the treasure, the hoarders were unwittingly preparing a comfortable nest where a tired serpent could curl up in comfort. Although many people experience a frisson of horror when they catch sight of a snake – possibly because of the primeval instinct to avoid a deathly bite – its association with buried treasure means that many Chinese have a tendency to regard the Snake as a harbinger of good fortune.

The Chinese associate the Snake with secrets and intrigue. Eavesdropping and espionage are associated with the Snake, and those born in the Snake year are good information gatherers. Intrigues, stratagems and scandals rarely pass by the Snake without being noted for future benefit. Unlike their more garrulous neighbours, however, Snake people like to keep such titbits of trivia to themselves, salting away snippets of information until a more fruitful opportunity arrives when they can be revealed in all their alarming intensity.

By their careful manipulation of circumstances, Snake people can rise to high positions of power, not through any outward displays of ambition and self-promotion, but by being able to be in precisely the right place at a time when their unparalleled skills are most needed. Facts and figures fall naturally into the Snake's understanding, and they make excellent researchers.

The Snake is very selective, and its partner has to offer something lacking in the Snake's life: earthy robustness, or exotic dazzle – it does not matter which. The Ox would provide the former quality, while the Rooster, or even the Dragon, would tingle the Snake with a frisson of illicit but glamorous intrigue. A Chinese proverb adds yet another prospective partner: 'When the Snake and Rabbit meet, there is true happiness.'

Snake people have a strict sense of morality and ethics. They are basically truthful, but if forced into revealing a confidence, they use their verbal dexterity to present facts with cosmetic adjustment. They can also give the impression that they know far more about something than can comfortably be divulged, certainly a useful ability during tricky commercial negotiations.

The Snake is an astute money manager, and will always be able to account for the last penny.

The Snake is essentially a private person, and its home is unlikely to be an open house. There may be a number of surprising treasures such as paintings that are not for general appreciation. The Snake is very sensuous, and will often indulge in luxuries which it considers to be of no concern to anyone else.

Snakes like to dress expensively but discreetly, for they dress not to impress others, but to remain as unobtrusive as possible.

THE HORSE

IN THE CHINESE CALENDAR, the Horse month marks the half-way point of the year, and includes the longest day, when the Sun, the Great Yang, is at its maximum power. Similarly, its hour is midday when, whatever the season, the Sun is at its height. Astrologers of old chose the Horse to represent the Great Yang, associated with men and their occupations out of doors.

Thus the Horse represents all things masculine, attitudes as well as attributes. Socializing, sport and macho banter are the typical signs of the Horse influence. For this reason, Chinese parents looking for a prospective daughter-in-law would feel uncomfortable about choosing a bride born in a Horse year as they would feel that such a girl would be the dominant partner in a marriage.

The male Horse likes to think that the two genders should lead distinctly separate lives, following their traditionally allocated tasks: the man working in the fields and bringing home the harvest; the woman labouring indoors as housewife and mother to his children. On the other hand, the female Horse is a champion of her sex, and holds the contrary view: as far as she is concerned, both partners in a relationship should share the responsibilities and duties of managing a household and, in return, receive the same remuneration and recognition for their contributions to it.

The Horse character is fundamentally both sociable and competitive, but inclined to be part of a team rather than an individual. The Horse may well be a fanatic or revolutionary, but only if everyone else is too, although with its qualities of leadership and forthright speaking, there will no problem in finding followers for its cause. Holding firm and entrenched views, the Horse is unlikely to be dissuaded from its opinions, the negative side of this being that the typical Horse can be prejudiced.

Horses and credit cards are not a good combination. Believing that its first priority is to create a positive impression, the Horse tends to behave rashly when managing its finances. It usually manages to balance its budget, even though it may mean cutting back on what others might regard as essentials.

The best match for a lifelong relationship is the Sheep, since Horse and Sheep represent the opposite qualities and the two sides of a partnership. Other favourable companions (provided that they do not get in the way) would be the Tiger, especially if the Horse is female, and the Dog, who would share the Horse's love of the outdoor or sporting life. Partners to avoid would be the Rat or Rabbit, while the Rooster would distract attention from the Horse, much to its chagrin. According to a Chinese proverb 'the Ox and Horse cannot share the same stall'.

Female Horses make good committee people, and are dedicated organizers. Whether it is an office outing to the countryside, a trade conference, or a family occasion, the female Horse is the right person to get the job done to the satisfaction of all concerned.

Although the superficial characteristics of the Horse personality relate to sport and physical activities, the underlying qualities will still be found in Horse people who are more cerebral or intellectual. They too enjoy the stimulation of mental challenges and the company of like-minded fellow puzzle-solvers, and are to be found occupying leading places in bridge, quiz and similar contests.

Although not a slavish follower of fashion, the Horse does not want to seem out of touch, and will opt for styles that are in vogue without being too distinctive.

THE SHEEP

THE COMPANION SIGN to the masculine Yang Horse is the Yin Sheep, these two signs representing the two aspects of the House of Gender. The Buddhist sages chose the Sheep to represent feminine qualities since flocks of sheep are almost exclusively female. In Chinese, the word for sheep is the same as that for goat, while it is sometimes translated as 'ram'.

The Sheep therefore represents a wide range of symbolic qualities: some people share its crowd-following nature. Others take after the less gregarious goat, preferring the company of just one or two chosen friends. But there are many qualities that are shared by all the Sheep types. One is the love of art forms such as singing or dancing, where the performer can be either part of a band or group, or a soloist. In the visual arts, the Sheep is more likely to be fond of drawings and pastels and muted shades rather than neo-modernist works in primary colours, and this taste will be reflected in the Sheep's home furnishings.

In close personal relationships, the Sheep symbolizes the forging of permanent bonds, particularly marriage. Not every Sheep gets drawn into the ideal relationship, however, and while the lone Sheep may appear self-sufficient and philosophical about its plight, it does not regard being single as a blessing. Family life has an important role, but it is the attached Sheep who is most likely to have strong family bonds.

Any career in which the Sheep can operate within a team framework suits the Sheep personality; a life in music or dancing may be the Sheep's secret choice, but a profession dealing with people, such as welfare or human resources, would seem the natural route for the Sheep to take.

The spirit of company and fellowship is so strong in the Sheep personality that they have an unfortunate disregard for the individuality of other people. The Sheep, seeing everyone else, whoever they are, as other Sheep, refuses to believe that colleagues and friends do not share the same enthusiasms, cheer the same team, or enjoy the same type of pizza. The first time they are faced with this revelation can be an upsetting experience for them, but the sooner this happens, the greater will be their understanding of people outside the close family circle.

IDEAL COMPANION

The strong family qualities associated with the Sheep show that its ideal partners are the domestic Pig or the caring Rabbit. Either of these will bring the Sheep the happiness of the companionship for which it yearns, however secretly. If the Sheep is happy to maintain a secondary position in a relationship, then the fiery Horse would be a fine stable-mate. The Rooster may hold some magnetic attraction for the Sheep, as would the Snake, but an Ox for a companion would lead to heartache and upset.

Conversely, however, the Sheep suffers this same fate at the hands of more emphatic colleagues, especially those who hold any position of authority. Such people may regard the Sheep as naive and pliable, taking their acquiescence for granted. However, to underestimate the Sheep's integrity is to invite disaster; pushed to extremes, the gentle Sheep becomes the hostile ram, with calamitous consequences.

The Sheep tends to look only at the surface of a situation, assuming that the details will sort themselves out. In business they succeed best when they are able to deal with people and things, and leave the intangibles in the capable hands of experts.

The Sheep's appearance is both reassuring and friendly, for it will always plump for an outfit that is both comfortable and attractive, which can be worn confidently straight from a business meeting to an evening engagement.

THE MONKEY

THE ANIMAL NAMES Monkey and Rooster have little to do with their ancient signs, but are based on their astrological interpretation. The two signs together comprise the skill and technology duo, the Yang quality representing technical expertise and heavy machinery, while the Yin counterpart is more concerned with design and handiwork.

On the Chinese clock the Monkey hour is the last working hour of the day, just before sunset. The ancient sign showed a leather hide being stretched on a frame, signifying someone stretching wearily.

The Monkey is a popular figure of Chinese legend, the mischievous hero of a classic tale who accompanied the monk Xuan Zang on his perilous journey to the West. In the epic, the Monkey embodies the essence of human nature and its frailties, which can, however, be redeemed through good works.

The astrological symbolism of the Monkey is a facility with words as well as deeds. Superficially, the Monkey represents the ability to fashion metal, from the minutest detail in the painstaking assembly of jewellery or watches, to the huge constructions of engines and bridges. The Monkey person who does not have gifted fingers will have a glib tongue, and some Monkey personalities will use their undoubted abilities in the law courts.

But the Monkey's skills, verbal or palpable, must be put to good use. The hands of one Monkey may be employed to perform delicate surgery; the hands of another will silently turn the tumblers of a bank safe. And an unsuspecting lawyer may be baffled to bewilderment by the crafty Monkey in the dock. As inventive as the Monkey is, its creations have to be considered with awe, for what may have begun as a way to improve life may turn out to be a complete catastrophe when it is misused.

The Monkey's finances are apt to be erratic. But there will be times of affluence; the secret lies in holding on to any gains.

When the Monkey is head of the household it is difficult to maintain a calm atmosphere since the younger members of the family follow the lead of their hyperactive parent. But there will usually be one member of the family who will act as a buttress during the occasional crisis.

With the Rat and the Dragon as companions, one as its partner in life, and the other as a friend or close family member, the Monkey can achieve phenomenal personal success and reach the heights of human happiness. Finding these two companions is the Monkey's quest. For a more modest life, the Horse will provide friendship, comfort and security for all its days, while a merry time can be had with the Dog. The Tiger is unlikely to prove an amenable companion.

When teamed up with the right people, with sufficient resources to hand, and a definite objective to follow, the Monkey sparkles into creative activity, throwing itself enthusiastically into ambitious schemes that gain admiration from all quarters. If the Monkey is wiser after all its experiences, it will refuse to allow the acclaim and good fortune it has attracted to overshadow its intrinsic nature but will, once again, begin to build the foundations of a scheme that will ultimately be of benefit to all.

In a crowd, the Monkey may give itself away by its penchant for the small and intricate, eschewing bold strokes or large expanses of colour. The small patterns, fine textures and delicate jewellery worn by the Monkey all reveal the basic traits of this complex character.

THE ROOSTER

WHAT A COMPLEX CHARACTER is the Rooster! This is partly revealed in the contradictory nature of the Rooster symbolism: although associated with the dawn alarm, the Chinese clock puts the Rooster at sunset, when the birds come back to roost.

So it is that the Rooster is associated with evening activities. Thus all kinds of artistic pursuits and entertainments – music, painting, reading, theatre, concerts and the like – fall under the influence of the Rooster.

Although the Rooster is a Yin or feminine sign, it is the most aggressively assertive of all the Yin signs, and has many of the Yang qualities of the authoritative Tiger. Roosters are talkers rather than conversationalists, and do not condescend to smooth the edges of their pronouncements. Their frank and outspoken manner can seem unnecessarily abrasive to others and is often misunderstood as rudeness.

In the home, this outspokenness means that there is no doubt who is in charge; pity the person who steps out of line. The Rooster may not be the titular head of the family, but is certainly the effective one.

Astrologically, the Rooster and money are almost synonymous. Although Roosters have a shrewd business sense, and are careful hoarders, they occasionally flout accepted budgeting conventions with shows of flagrant extravagance. The female Rooster is more likely to bring money in; the male is more adept at disposing of it.

Anxious to be the first to hear or relay the latest news, Roosters have all the qualities needed to make good journalists and magazine writers. Whatever career the Rooster is drawn to, those aspects of their work that have a feminine slant to them will be more prosperous.

Like the farmyard Rooster, those born under this astrological sign are early risers, active and alert long before the rest of the household, and can usually manage with less sleep than the average person. They may express an anxiety about this, thinking perhaps that their metabolism is awry, but it is not a problem if they are able to adjust their daily lives accordingly. Yet there is one factor of their daily life that does have to be watched carefully; it is revealed by the ancient symbol of the wine bottle. The appearance of one Rooster in the overall horoscope is not an unfavourable sign, but when a second or third appears, in the hour, day, or month, it can be a warning against becoming reliant on alcohol, drugs or other substances, whether for medical reasons or for recreation.

Rooster people are proud, and always like to create a good impression. They need to be fashionable, following the latest styles and keen to be familiar with the latest trends, yet they will shun anything that is outrageously daring, or that would draw attention for the wrong reasons. They require admiration, not amazement. Fastidious to the point of obsession, if they perceive the slightest flaw in their appearance, dress or make-up, no matter how insignificant, it is not merely an embarrassment for them, it actually evokes a frigid horror which less sensitive people may fail to understand.

IDEAL COMPANION

Who would take on such an unpredictable but stimulating personality? It has to be someone who lacks the qualities it most admires in the Rooster, even though others may find these the least attractive sides of the Rooster's character. The steady, trustworthy Ox is one such partner, the quiet and reserved Snake another. The Sheep or the Pig would provide a comfortable home. The Tiger, the Horse or another Rooster would provide too much competition, and neither would know who is the star.

THE DOG

In ancient Chinese writings, the sign that we now know as the Dog showed a hand holding a spear. It indicated the time of the day when the homestead was secured for the night, and a watchman put on duty. With its determination, bravery and fortitude the Dog was the obvious choice to represent this function of security and defence.

Together, the Dog and the Pig are the companion signs ruling over the house and home – the Dog being in charge of the security of the outside walls, the Pig the comforts within. Thus the Dog is concerned not just with the security and safety of the home, but with the material construction of the house itself. In some Dog personalities, this is revealed by an interest in buildings, not as homes so much as investments. The Dog prefers not to rent, but to buy, being inclined to move frequently, always into larger properties with greater potential for improvement.

The Dog month is the End of Summer, when the harvest is gathered. The Dog is inclined to be a saver, and can make sacrifices when there is something to be achieved, perhaps through having already experienced a lean time in the past. Being a hard worker and used to making the best of the prevailing circumstances, the Dog can tolerate conditions that would cause others to flinch.

The defensive nature of the Dog makes a faithful and trusted friend. Such people are inherently suspicious of strangers, but once an attachment is made, will stay loyal no matter what difficulties or strains are put on the friendship. They will always lend a hand, quietly and without fuss. They like to volunteer their services, either to help a friend, or in the service of some good cause. It is not surprising that they make friends easily, but they can be too trusting at times. Unscrupulous acquaintances or even family members all too often take advantage of their good nature. When the Dog is warned about the behaviour and questionable activities of people who are supposed to be close, such advice is shrugged off with unconcern. But although usually affable and casual, Dog people can be stirred to sudden anger when faced with an unpardonable affront.

Dogs like the home to be a haven, clean and tidy. In the family things are likely to be directed from the top, with fragile links between parents and children.

Dogs love the outdoors, and are fond of country pursuits and sporting activities. It is important to choose a partner who is inclined to share this fondness for fresh air or is willing to let the Dog follow its own agenda.

In choosing a career, military service and security roles are alluded to in the old sign of the hand and spear. Property dealing and building and restoration work are also very close to the Dog's inherent nature, but there should always be opportunities for outdoor work; being shut in a confined factory or office setting would eventually lead to depression.

There is a touch of the sensible and practical in the Dog's appearance; the female is likely to prefer a 'power-dressing' style, while the male favours a playful touch. In either case the aim is to present an air of businesslike camaraderie.

IDEAL COMPANION

The Dog feels a close alliance with the Tiger and the Horse, and since they have many interests in common, either will form a lasting and sociable friendship with the Dog. The Pig is the more domestic counterpart to the Dog's outgoing nature, but both will have to learn to understand the needs of the other. The Ox is likely to prove cantankerous and sullen in time, while the Dragon may run off with all the Dog's money!

THE PIG

THE CHINESE SIGN that was used before the animal names were invented is said to represent two people in bed under a roof. The Pig was probably adopted for the last of the 12 ancient Chinese signs because it represented the last hours of the Chinese day, when the family had gone to sleep, and all that could be heard was the gentle snoring of a household at peace with itself.

Some newcomers to Chinese astrology, having learnt that the Animal Zodiac includes such exotic creatures as the Tiger and the Dragon, might feel deflated if they were told that they were humble Pigs. But the true Pig character wouldn't mind at all. For Pig personalities belong to one of the pleasantest types of people it is possible to meet. They are friendly, warm, generous and jovial.

Far from living in squalor, as might be thought from the derogatory meaning of 'pigsty', the Pig personality's home is comfortable, often even luxurious, and welcoming. Although the Pig is not assertive by nature, and may have a subordinate role in the family hierarchy, the household will yield to its unspoken authority on domestic arrangements. There is always a comfortable chair to sit on, and though the house may be scrupulously clean, visitors are never so intimidated by orderliness that they feel afraid to put a foot down in the wrong place.

But comfort costs, and to finance the lifestyle to which the Pig would like to be accustomed requires lots of hard work. Those outside the Pig's close circle may think the Pig to be exceptionally lucky where money is concerned, but although there will be the occasional welcome windfall apples, the Pig's agreeable environment is really due to sheer industriousness. When the Pig happens to be in the right place at the right time, this is not through happy chance, but careful planning.

But the Pig's friendliness and apparent carefree attitude do have their drawbacks. In trying to please everyone, the Pig's accommodating nature gets taken for granted. The Pig should bear in mind the old proverb – it is hard enough to be charitable, but even harder to stop. The Pig may often be deceived, especially in money matters. When the Pig loses money, it is not through failed business ventures, but in trying to support causes that were lost from the outset.

The careers that suit the Pig personality therefore tend to be associated with the service industries: home furnishings, interior design, hotel management and anything that has a five-star quality about it. Other professions in which the Pig's natural aptitudes are likely to find fulfilment are the welfare services and caring for the aged or infirm.

The Pig likes to dress as fashionably as its budget allows, and although comfort and practicality are its first considerations, there will always be a notable element of stylishness that others may envy, but would be reluctant to copy too closely.

IDEAL COMPANION

Sadly, the Pig is not a good judge of character, and is often drawn to unlikely partnerships with the wrong people. The Pig's ideal partner would be either the Rabbit or the Sheep, both of whom share the same commitment to home and family. When the Pig is female, a Dog would be an ideal match as someone having a similar interest in home improvements. If the Pig is male, he might be attracted to the flamboyant Rooster, though the Rooster's expensive tastes could make an unwelcome incursion into his budget!

THE ANIMAL SIGN FOR THE MONTH

In ancient times, Chinese farmers and fishermen would study natural occurrences such as the return or departure of migrating birds, fish and animals, or the blossoming of flowers to know which month they were in. 'In the first month, the insects waken; the wild geese go to their northern lands, and the moles come out', runs an ancient Chinese text. If these natural events were seen to be happening all around them then the first month of the year had arrived; if not, spring was still waiting in the wings.

Since the beginning of recorded time, the Chinese divided the year into months, each one beginning with the New Moon. Unfortunately, a year based on 12 New Moons has only 354 days. Unless some adjustment were made to the calendar, the New Year would get earlier and earlier each year until eventually, after 15 years, the seasons would be reversed. To compensate for the shortfall, every few years an extra 'moon' was added so that some years had 13 'moons'. Watching out for the wild geese on their annual journey to the

MONTHLY ANIMAL SIGNS

FROM	TO	ANIMAL SIGN	see page
7 December	5 January	Rat	52
6 January	3 February	Ox	52
4 February	5 March	Tiger	53
6 March	4 April	Rabbit	53
5 April	5 May	Dragon	54
6 May	5 June	Snake	54
6 June	6 July	Horse	55
7 July	7 August	Sheep	55
8 August	7 September	Monkey	56
8 September	7 October	Rooster	56
8 October	7 November	Dog	57
8 November	6 December	Pig	57

northern lands, or waiting for the mole or groundhog to come out was one way of knowing if an extra month had to be added. When the techniques of astronomy became more exact, this ancient but quaint method of measuring the year was replaced by the more scientific method of making the New Year the second New Moon after the shortest day.

THE LUNAR AND SOLAR CALENDARS

Although some astrologers use the lunar months in their calculations, most follow the old imperial practice, a combination of the lunar and solar calendars. The solar calendar divides the Sun's year into 12 months which run parallel with the Western zodiacal signs, the difference being that each Chinese solar month starts with the middle of one zodiacal sign, and finishes with the middle of the next. Thus, the first Chinese month, which begins with the Beginning of Spring, starts in the

THE RETURN OF THE WILD GEESE
Returning geese herald the arrival of spring. In Chinese literature this beautiful metaphor is often used to mean homecoming.

middle of Aquarius, and ends in the middle of Pisces. Similarly, the second Chinese month runs from early March to early April, with the Spring Equinox, the start of Aries, as its middle point. Each Chinese month begins, approximately, on the same Western date every year but, like the Beginning of Spring, advances by one day every 70 years or so.

For a quick search for your monthly Animal Sign, use the table on page 48, which is valid for all dates except those that are close to the end or beginning of the Chinese solar month. As there are slight changes in some years, any dates either side of the ones listed in the table of Monthly Animal Signs should be checked in the supplementary table on pages 140–1 that lists the dates of the solar months.

THE ANIMALS
AND THE SEASONS

Traditional Chinese astrologers pay great attention to the season in which a person is born, and of course this is revealed by the month itself. The shortest day always occurs in the middle of the Rat month, the longest day in the Horse month, while the middle of the Rabbit and Rooster months mark the times when the days and nights are of equal length. So in the Chinese calendar, the Rat, Rabbit, Horse and Rooster represent winter, spring, summer and autumn respectively.

The four months that come before these signify the approach of the seasons: so that the Pig month (which comes before the Rat month in the Chinese calendar) is the Approach of Winter; the Tiger is the Approach of Spring; the

Snake is the Approach of Summer, and the Monkey is the Approach of Autumn.

You might think that the month that followed the seasonal months would be called the Passing of Summer, or whatever, but this is not the case. Instead, the Chinese insert a fifth season, the Earth season, which is a fallow or waiting period before the approach of the next season. This means that the Ox, Dragon, Sheep and Dog months are known as Earth months.

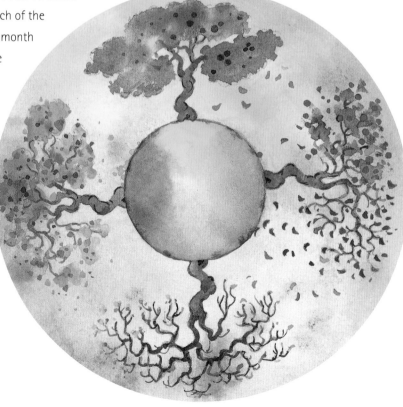

THE SEASONS

Chinese painters attach great importance to the symbolism of the seasons. Whether a tree is blooming or leafless can suggest hidden emotions.

HOW THE SEASONAL ANIMALS AFFECT THE HOROSCOPE

The month generates the day. In the Chinese horoscope, the day factors represent the subject – the person for whom the horoscope is cast – and the month those people who are responsible for the subject's welfare. The subject's relations with the parents who brought the child into the world, the teachers who provided knowledge, or the employers who provide the means of a livelihood, are revealed by the month, or seasonal, animal.

Whether the relationship is favourable or not depends on whether the seasons follow naturally, or are in opposition. Thus, winter gives rise to spring, so that these two seasons are in a favourable relationship. If the month animal were a Tiger (the Approach of Spring), and the day animal were a Horse (summer), it could be said that the parents were supportive, since spring moves into summer. But winter and summer oppose; spring and autumn oppose. If the month animal were a Rabbit, and the day animal were a Rooster, because these two seasons are opposite to each other, it could reveal a lack of closeness and understanding between subject and parents.

When the month and day animals are both Earth, as would be the case if the horoscope had an Ox month and a Sheep day, then there would be neither strong attachment nor hostility, since an Earth animal generally represents a stable, detached relationship.

The symbolism for each monthly Animal Sign derives from the season to which it

Here are the 12 months according to their Animal Signs, and the seasons of the year that they rule:

7 December	Rat	Winter
6 January	Ox	Earth
4 February	Tiger	Approach of Spring
6 March	Rabbit	Spring
5 April	Dragon	Earth
6 May	Snake	Approach of Summer
6 June	Horse	Summer
7 July	Sheep	Earth
8 August	Monkey	Approach of Autumn
8 September	Rooster	Autumn
8 October	Dog	Earth
8 November	Pig	Approach of Winter

belongs. When the monthly sign belongs to a season that generates the daily sign, the qualities of the older generation will be admired and passed down to the subject, but if the two Animal Signs belong to opposite seasons, then the subject will be determined not to repeat the mistakes of the parents. This observation may additionally refer to the way that the subject perceives teachers, lawyers or other people in authoritative positions.

In judging the quality of the relationship between the subject and the older generation, first take into account the nature of each of the monthly Animal Signs, then see whether they harmonize with the daily Animal Signs.

RAT
WINsrvdTER

*'The ice thickens,
and the dawn herald
no longer crows.'*

The Rat month includes the shortest
day when we become aware that winter
is upon us, with worse to come. There is
still time for last-minute merrymaking
before the cold months ahead demand
a period of economy and strict
budgeting. The parents are not without
a sense of humour, but may appear to
be moralistic and disciplinarian. The
attitude towards employers is one of
friendly respect.

OX
EARTH

*'Wild geese travel
northwards and birds of prey
become ferocious.'*

The Ox month is in deepest winter,
when many animals are hibernating
and plants are sleeping and waiting for
the spring. Although it is a period of
restraint and watchfulness, there are
better days ahead. The subject's parents
may seem cold and distant, but there is
much love even if it is not always
expressed openly. People in authority
or management seem to be distant
and unapproachable.

TIGER
APPROACH OF SPRING

'The wind warms the frost,
and sleeping insects
begin to move.'

At once there is a spirit of optimism;
plans are made for the coming year.
Parents are enthusiastic and ambitious.
The subject enjoys working for people
with grand ideas for expansion and
development. The first signs of a thaw
and the green shoots of snowdrops
pushing their way through the melting
snow herald the Approach of Spring.

RABBIT
SPRING

'Peach trees blossom
and the oriole sings.'

Spring is already here, and there is
much to be done. It is time to cast away
the old and worn, and to rebuild with
vigour. It is a sign of revolutionary
ideas. Parents are energetic and vital,
restless and constantly wanting to
change. The subject will aim to work for
people who strive for the new and have
no time for old-established traditions.

DRAGON
EARTH

'Rainbows are seen,
and duckweed begins
to cover the water.'

The rain may be uncomfortable, but it is needed to water the coming crops. Yet when too much rain falls, floods can be disastrous. Thus there are material benefits to be had, but greed will bring grief. The attitude towards parents is that they seem to be too busy making money to realize that they are losing touch with the things that really matter.

SNAKE
APPROACH OF SUMMER

'Green frogs croak
and melons ripen.'

There is much to enjoy in life, but to enjoy leisure it is necessary to work hard. It signifies a busy life spent acquiring wealth, but little time to enjoy it. The subject may envy his parents' sound financial position without appreciating the amount of hard work and sacrifice that has gone into getting there.

HORSE
SUMMER

*'The mantis appears
and the magpie cries.'*

In the hot summer days, it seems that
nature has bestowed its blessings
copiously, and there is little to do but
enjoy its burgeoning abundance. It is a
sign of a carefree, easy lifestyle, with
few responsibilities, or perhaps a
disregard of them. (Exceptionally, it is
unfavourable when the Horse passes
these qualities to an Earth season
animal, other than the Dog.)

SHEEP
EARTH

*'The cricket
sits in the walls, and the
glow-worms shine.'*

The cricket's chirp is a warning that it is
time to look to the future. Despite the
apparent prosperity of the moment, it is
wise to remember that there have been
and perhaps will be hard times. For the
subject who has not experienced the
tribulations of the past, the careful
parent appears to be over-anxious.
Such subjects tend to criticize their
employer's apparent meanness.

MONKEY
APPROACH OF AUTUMN

*'A cool wind blows
and white frost forms.'*

Summer days are coming to an end. Preparations must be made to gather the harvest before the frosts begin to bite. Houses must be repaired and made secure while the days are still warm enough to work outside. The Monkey month denotes people who are industrious and busy, and who like to be constructively occupied. Such parents are admired by their children.

ROOSTER
AUTUMN

*'On stormy winds the
wild geese come,
and swallows return south.'*

As one arrives, another one goes. The child may recall changes in family circumstances, such as a parent's second marriage, or moving house. The Autumn Equinox marks the time of lengthening nights, indicating that the changes are not always happy. At work, the subject will be encumbered by constant reorganization of management and policy.

DOG
EARTH

*'Geese call on their
way home, and the
yellow leaves fall.'*

There is an urgency to depart; the
benefits of the present situation have
been exhausted. This signifies a parent
who is often away from the house,
for business commitments or other
reasons. Nevertheless, it results in a
sense of loss or loneliness. The subject
is likely to be drawn into a profession
that demands long periods of absence
from home.

PIG
APPROACH OF WINTER

*'Water freezes
and there are
no more rainbows.'*

The Approach of Winter reveals a
frugal side which closely borders on
pessimism. The good things in life
either belong to the past or the future,
but certainly not the present. The
subject may look back on childhood
with some regret at not having been
able to enjoy the things that today's
children take for granted. Employers
will be regarded as parsimonious.

THE ANIMAL SIGN FOR THE DAY

Unlike the Animal Sign for the year and the month, the Animal Sign for the day does not depend on the motions of the Sun, Moon, or Earth, but follows a regularly repeating sequence of 60 days, without any regard to the year or seasons.

To find the Animal Sign for the day, use the calculations given on page 60; they need no further amendment.

The Animal Sign for the Day is another name for what is properly called the 'branch' of the day. This is one of a pair of numbers that were used by ancient soothsayers at the dawn of civilization in China. In those distant days, shamans consulting their oracles scratched their questions on animal bones, and later, noted whether or not the prediction was correct. But, significantly, they also recorded the day when the oracle was consulted, sometimes with the month, and in nearly every case with two code numbers known as the Heavenly Stem and the Earthly Branch. These bone oracles constitute the oldest examples of Chinese writing.

The 'stems' were originally the names of the days of a ten-day week. They were probably the names of ancient gods whose functions have now been lost and forgotten. However, the fifth sign shows a hand holding a spear, so

it may have been the ancient Chinese equivalent of Mars, god of battle. The eighth represented a flower or herb (in modern Chinese it means 'bitter') which suggests it might have been dedicated to the god of medicine. But the tenth is the most interesting: nearly every oracle bone inscription begins with this sign, implying that it was a day reserved for divination, prayer and sacrifice.

For greater precision, the days were also numbered by another parallel set of 12 names, the branches, which originally marked the 12 two-hour periods in a day. When the ten stems are combined with the 12 branches it produces a cycle of 60 possible pairs of numbers (not 120, as might be thought, because odd-numbered stems could only be paired with odd-numbered branches, and even with even.)

In the past hundred years, hoards of these 'oracle bones' have been found inscribed with literally thousands of examples of the stem-and-branch dates. So regular and so accurate is stem-and-branch counting that when archaeologists discover bronzes and other items inscribed with stem-and-branch dates, they are often able to say with absolute precision when the objects were made. Today's astronomers have been able to use ancient observations of eclipses and other celestial phenomena to build up a picture of how the universe evolved.

In CE 13, the official court historians decided that the stems and branches would be a convenient way to number the years as well. Until then years were marked by the length of time the current emperor had been on the throne. Now, astrologers use the stem-and-branches to mark not only the years and days but the months and hours as well.

Most of this book is concerned only with the meaning of the Earthly Branches, that is, the 12 Animal Signs. But the Stem of the day, by far the oldest part of the Chinese horoscope, has a special importance. That is why this section, concerning the Animal Sign for the day, gives each of the 60 daily stem-and-branch combinations individually.

ECLIPSES OF THE SUN
Because they can occur only at the New Moon, eclipses of the Sun were a sure means of regulating the complex Chinese calendar precisely.

TO FIND THE ANIMAL SIGN FOR THE DAY

To find the Animal Sign for the DAY you just need to add three numbers together. While this is a little more complicated than finding the Animal Sign for the year or the month there is one decided advantage: this calculation is valid for any day in any year.

Many Chinese people look in their calendars to find the Animal Sign for the day in order to establish whether the day will be favourable for them. For example, an Ox day might suggest that they will have to work hard, a Dragon day that it is going to be lucky for them – or unlucky, if their own Animal Sign happens to be a Dog!

EXAMPLE

What is the Animal Sign for someone born on 3 January 1988?

❶ From Table A, the code number for 1988 (January/February column) is 51.

❷ From Table B, the code number for January is 0.

❸ For the third day add 3.

Total: $51 + 0 + 3 = 54$

❹ Result: 54.

❺ From Table C the daily Animal Sign for 54 is Snake.

HOW TO DO IT

❶ From Table A, find the required year and note its code number. As leap years change the code number after the end of February, they have two code numbers: one for January and February, the other for the months from March to December.

❷ From Table B, find the code number for the Western calendar month of birth.

❸ Add the code numbers for the year and month to the figure for the date (3 January would be 3).

❹ If the total is more than 120, subtract 120; if it's more than 60, subtract 60.

❺ The Animal Sign for the day is shown in Table C. To find out what the Animal Sign for the day reveals, see pages 63–9.

TABLE A: CODE NUMBERS FOR THE YEARS

			Jan/Feb	Mar/Dec				Jan/Feb	Mar/Dec
1917 39	1918 44	1919 49	1920 54	1920 55	1921 0	1922 5	1923 10	1924 15	1924 16
1925 21	1926 26	1927 31	1928 36	1928 37	1929 42	1930 47	1931 52	1932 57	1932 58
1933 3	1934 8	1935 13	1936 18	1936 19	1937 24	1938 29	1939 34	1940 39	1940 40
1941 45	1942 50	1943 55	1944 0	1944 1	1945 6	1946 11	1947 16	1948 21	1948 22
1949 27	1950 32	1951 37	1952 42	1952 43	1953 48	1954 53	1955 58	1956 3	1956 4
1957 9	1958 14	1959 19	1960 24	1960 25	1961 30	1962 35	1963 40	1964 45	1964 46
1965 51	1966 56	1967 1	1968 6	1968 7	1969 12	1970 17	1971 22	1972 27	1972 28
1973 33	1974 38	1975 43	1976 48	1976 49	1977 54	1978 59	1979 4	1980 9	1980 10
1981 15	1982 20	1983 25	1984 30	1984 31	1985 36	1986 41	1987 46	1988 51	1988 52
1989 57	1990 2	1991 7	1992 12	1992 13	1993 18	1994 23	1995 28	1996 33	1996 34
1997 39	1998 44	1999 49	2000 54	2000 55	2001 0	2002 5	2003 10	2004 15	2004 16
2005 21	2006 26	2007 31	2008 36	2008 37	2009 42	2010 47	2011 52	2012 57	2012 58
2013 3	2014 8	2015 13	2016 18	2016 19	2017 24	2018 29	2019 34	2020 39	2020 40
2021 45	2022 50	2023 55	2024 0	2024 1	2025 6	2026 11	2027 16	2028 21	2028 22

TABLE B: CODE NUMBERS FOR THE MONTHS

Jan	Feb	Mar	Apr	May	Jun	Jul	Aug	Sept	Oct	Nov	Dec
0	31	59	30	0	31	1	32	3	33	4	34

TABLE C: ANIMAL SIGNS FOR THE 60-DAY CYCLE

1	2	3	4	5	6	7	8	9	10	11	12
13	14	15	16	17	18	19	20	21	22	23	24
25	26	27	28	29	30	31	32	33	34	35	36
37	38	39	40	41	42	43	44	45	46	47	48
49	50	51	52	53	54	55	56	57	58	59	60
Rat	Ox	Tiger	Rabbit	Dragon	Snake	Horse	Sheep	Monkey	Rooster	Dog	Pig

STEM AND BRANCH

The daily number, or stem and branch for the day, gives a general indication of the prospects for people born on that day, and the kinds of obstacles they have to face in life. The daily number gives you more than just the Animal Sign for the day, but when constructing the horoscope chart, you only need to use the Animal Sign.

The daily number can also be used for a daily prediction, or to get advice regarding the suitability of a chosen date for a particular event or transaction. Find the daily number for the required day, following exactly the same method as that given on page 60.

The headings for each of the explanations of the 60 stem-and-branch signs begin with the number (1 to 60) found from the calculation on page 60. This is followed by the stem and branch expressed as a number from 1 to 10 (the stem), and as a roman numeral from I to XII (the branch).

As many Western writers (and Chinese authors writing for a Western readership) refer to the stems by the names of the Five Elements of Chinese philosophy, these have been included in brackets.

The equivalent Animal Sign for the branch follows, together with the traditional popular name for each of the different animal types, although these are not found in the classic astrology texts. They are usually applied to each cycle of 60 years, but have been included here as they also give a guide to the interpretation of each stem and branch.

1 STEM 1 (YANG WOOD) BRANCH I RAT ON THE ROOF

The Stem 1 (Yang Wood) Rat shows great sensitivity allied with an active creative mind. Hidden artistic talents may have to be kept concealed. But there will be a chance to put ideas forward eventually. Leadership qualities will ensure admiration and success.

2 STEM 2 (YIN WOOD) BRANCH II OX ON THE SHORE

Resolution is coupled with a determination to succeed. Although the highest position will not be reached, it is possible to get very close. Jealous rivals will prevent the ultimate goal being achieved.

3 STEM 3 (YANG FIRE) BRANCH III TIGER IN THE FOREST

The skilful manipulator dissolves into the background. Through cunning and strategy and by keeping one's true strengths concealed, power and success are achieved.

4 STEM 4 (YIN FIRE) BRANCH IV RABBIT DREAMING OF THE MOON

The Rabbit of legend gazed at the Moon and was transported there, where he can still be seen, mixing the ingredients for the Elixir of Life. If dreams are sufficiently vivid and the details clearly recalled, it is possible to recreate them, so transmuting the picture into reality.

5 STEM 5 (YANG EARTH) BRANCH V DRAGON OF PURE VIRTUE

Those who strive to keep to the path of virtue will attain the highest honour. Defending those who are unable to act for themselves, and refusing to ignore wrongdoing, even though it may be disadvantageous to oneself, will eventually bring its rewards.

6 STEM 6 (YIN EARTH) BRANCH VI SNAKE OF HAPPINESS

It is a great blessing to be able to stimulate joy and laughter, and raise the spirits of those who are in greatest need of help. Achieving this does not require money or possessions. A quiet contented life is always envied by those whose riches become a burden of care and anxiety.

7 STEM 7 (YANG METAL) BRANCH VII HORSE AT THE PALACE

Although the position that is occupied in life may be a humble one, a chain of circumstances will bring this person into contact with the highest in the land. Fulfilling one's duties and responsibilities with a steady perseverance will be rewarded handsomely in later life.

8 STEM 8 (YIN METAL) BRANCH VIII SHEEP OF GOOD FORTUNE

There are great benefits to be gained and favours to be received by meeting people and making new contacts. It is unnecessary to strive for attention, for others will speak kindly and with respect. A life full of happiness and good health is promised for the future. Any gestures of friendship that are made, however small and seemingly insignificant, will be long remembered by the beneficiaries.

9 STEM 9 (YANG WATER) BRANCH IX MONKEY IN ELEGANT ATTIRE

Fine words and an ingratiating manner may not charm everyone, but those who manage these attributes to their maximum potential find that they are in a position to endow life with its finer qualities. Keep a close eye on the budget and beware of living beyond your means. Show kindness to those who are in a less fortunate position than yourself.

10 STEM 10 (YIN WATER) BRANCH X ROOSTER IN THE FARMYARD

A small but admiring crowd may be impressed by high talk, yet behind the superficial mask there are spiritual qualities that are seldom revealed. This person has the ability to look into the Golden Mirror to reveal future events.

11 STEM 1 (YANG WOOD) BRANCH XI DOG ON GUARD

The ever-watchful guard must remain alert; but when there is little to do, the mind becomes inventive. This is a person whose creative intellect is not used to the full.

12 STEM 2 (YIN WOOD) BRANCH XII PIG ON A JOURNEY

The Pig was the faithful companion of the Monk Xuan Zang who travelled to India to bring the Buddhist scriptures back to China. This sign symbolizes a pilgrimage, or travelling for a charitable purpose, rather than for reasons of business or pleasure.

13 STEM 3 (YANG FIRE) BRANCH I RAT IN THE FIELD

Some issues are more worthy than earning a comfortable living or raising a family. But while there are many things that have to be done in this life, there are few people willing to do them. Conscience and moral responsibility are of greater value than self-interest.

14 STEM 4 (YIN FIRE) BRANCH II OX IN THE LAKE

Sometimes, the pressures of everyday life become so great that the only solution is to get away from family, work and an oppressive environment. It is rarely possible to get what is wanted, so, as it is much easier to want what can be achieved, aspirations should be modified.

15 STEM 5 (YANG EARTH) BRANCH III TIGER CLIMBS THE MOUNTAIN

This sign shows resolution of purpose. There are many obstacles to be overcome, but strength of purpose will defeat all enemies. The eventual goal will be reached, and those who strive to hinder your progress will be defeated. Be diplomatic, since those who have been opposing your plans could be of assistance in the future.

16 STEM 6 (YIN EARTH) BRANCH IV RABBIT OF WOODS AND MOUNTAINS

It is better to have many places to go, instead of being obliged to remain in one spot. Opportunity is not going to call; it lies concealed and must be sought out. Those who are adventurous and unafraid of novel situations will make many influential friends.

17 STEM 7 (YANG METAL) BRANCH V DRAGON OF PATIENCE

Wisdom is achieved by listening, not by speaking. By waiting for the opportune moment it will be possible to benefit greatly, but if actions are too impetuous, all will be lost. Plan first, act later.

18 STEM 8 (YIN METAL) BRANCH VI SNAKE IN HIBERNATION

Often a great deal is achieved by doing nothing. Once seeds have been planted, do not dig them up to see if they are growing; they will do so of their own accord. Similarly, once plans are laid, they can be left to mature.

19 STEM 9 (YANG WATER) BRANCH VII HORSE AT WAR

When engaged in a dispute, it is important to have all the facts at hand. There is no point in quarrelling merely for the sake of winning an argument; there has to be a reasonable objective and a practical gain.

20 STEM 10 (YIN WATER) BRANCH VIII SHEEP IN THE FLOCK

Despite being surrounded by crowds, this person will always find time to sit quietly and meditate. A number of curious experiences seems to suggest that there are worlds beyond this one.

21 STEM 1 (YANG WOOD) BRANCH IX MONKEY IN A TREE

Up a tree, the creative Monkey is exactly where it should be. Ideas are sound and well thought out. It is now time to put them to the test. When the various possibilities are carefully considered, the correct solution soon becomes obvious.

22 STEM 2 (YIN WOOD) BRANCH X ROOSTER CROWING AT NOON

The proposal is constructed soundly, but will not be welcomed. Much work will be wasted if the results are presented at the wrong time. It is important that careful consideration is given to the matter of deciding when would be the most appropriate occasion for introducing the topic.

23 STEM 3 (YANG FIRE) BRANCH XI DOG ASLEEP

Everyone has to take a rest; it is folly to overwork those who need to be alert at all times. As people, so machinery. Even the most reliable of contrivances will break down eventually. Be prepared for such contingencies.

24 STEM 4 (YIN FIRE) BRANCH XII PIG CROSSES THE MOUNTAIN

Despite the task getting no easier, and the obstacles still to be overcome, there remains a steadfast determination to succeed. There can be no turning back, nor can the present course be abandoned. Struggle on, for the eventual rewards will be great.

25 STEM 5 (YANG EARTH) BRANCH I RAT IN THE GRANARY

There is a rich store of provisions, but all must be protected and defended against thieves. False friends and others who habitually court disaster must be abandoned. It is time to take a firm stand against the pleas for help and assistance, otherwise your savings will never accumulate.

26 STEM 6 (YIN EARTH) BRANCH II OX IN THE BYRE

All is in its rightful place. The plans being made will be successful. Much is to be gained by organizing family matters so that there is no conflict of interest between home and business.

27 STEM 7 (YANG METAL) BRANCH III TIGER LEAVES THE MOUNTAIN

Having made an important decision, it is now time to act. Because there are several problems that need to be resolved before it will be possible to go ahead with the new plans, it is vital to face up to those who had originally opposed the idea.

28 STEM 8 (YIN METAL) BRANCH IV RABBIT IN THE BURROW

Much can be achieved at home with family help without leaving the house. Success need not be measured in the amount of land one has, for the greater the size of the estate, the greater the responsibilities and stress.

29 STEM 9 (YANG WATER) BRANCH V DRAGON BRINGING RAIN

The rain brought by the Dragon symbolizes the benefits and rewards that are due, and that can now be enjoyed at last. Past services and loyalty will finally be rewarded, and many other benefits will follow.

30 STEM 10 (YIN WATER) BRANCH VI SNAKE IN THE GRASS

It is best to remain hidden, and not let your plans be known. There are many secrets that you cannot tell, for fear of being scorned. Experiences of spiritual insight should only be discussed with people who have a proper understanding of these matters.

31 STEM 1 (YANG WOOD) BRANCH VII HORSE IN THE CLOUDS

The imagination conceives a great plan, but there is no reason why it should remain a dream. With sufficient determination, and constant application, all the practical problems can be solved. There are those who declare that the ambition is impossible, but the faint-hearted can be proved wrong.

32 STEM 2 (YIN WOOD) BRANCH VIII SHEEP OF SERIOUS ASPECT

Constant practice and diligent application to the task are reward enough. A time for thought and investigation, rather than rash action.

33 STEM 3 (YANG FIRE) BRANCH IX MONKEY ON THE MOUNTAIN

The Monkey was another of Xuan Zang's companions (see No. 12, Pig on a Journey), but for most of the time, instead of helping, he played tricks and got up to mischief. But when faced with serious obstacles, the Monkey could provide valuable help. A time to cast away a carefree life, and attend to matters of more serious concern.

34 STEM 4 (YIN FIRE) BRANCH X ROOSTER IN SOLITUDE

Being a leader is never easy; it is important to keep a distance from tale-bearers and sycophants, and not to show favouritism. This may reduce the circle of friends, but it is the wisest course. There is still much you can do to improve your position. Do not let your pride prevent you from asking for advice. It is no shame to admit to ignorance.

35 STEM 5 (YANG EARTH) BRANCH XI DOG ON THE MOUNTAIN

Such a person tends to be cynical and suspicious of strangers, almost wanting to build a stronghold against invaders. There is so much that can be achieved in life, but before any ambitions can be realized, there are many battles to be won.

36 STEM 6 (YIN EARTH) BRANCH XII PIG IN THE MONASTERY

It may seem that the objective has been reached, but this is merely the half-way point. All the business of dismantling remains; after the congratulations, farewells have to be said, services to be paid, and the debris that was made on the way must now be cleared.

37 STEM 7 (YANG METAL) BRANCH I
RAT ON THE CROSSBEAM

Not in the granary full of rich provisions, but looking down on it from above, this is a picture of what might be. The rewards will not come of their own accord, you must go to them. It is a moment to make a decision.

38 STEM 8 (YIN METAL) BRANCH II
OX ON THE ROAD

There is advantage to be gained in travelling and constant movement. If health is a problem, a change of climate will be of benefit, as will vegetarian food.

39 STEM 9 (YANG WATER) BRANCH III
TIGER LEAVING THE FOREST

This is a dangerous moment; in the forest the Tiger was concealed; its stripes providing camouflage. Now the Tiger leaves, and may itself be hunted. It is a sign to be circumspect, warning that in leaving the present situation there are hidden perils ahead.

40 STEM 10 (YIN WATER) BRANCH IV
RABBIT LEAVING THE FOREST

There will come a time when it will be felt best to leave the towns and cities, and find a location in the countryside that is suitable for peaceful contemplation. It is good to practise the healing arts.

41 STEM 1 (YANG WOOD) BRANCH V
DRAGON IN THE WHIRLPOOL

Soon there will be an opportunity to meet with a person of great authority. It will not be an easy meeting; many unexpected questions will be asked, and it is important not to falter or show nervousness. If the preparation is sound, the result will be successful.

42 STEM 2 (YIN WOOD) BRANCH VI
SNAKE LEAVING A HOLE

A period of difficulties seems to be at an end, and it appears to be a good moment to make a new beginning. But while the time is favourable for expansion, it is always wise to be cautious, and avoid taking risks.

43 STEM 3 (YANG FIRE) BRANCH VII
HORSE MAKING A JOURNEY

Much can be achieved through travel, whether this is undertaken for business or pleasure. Many companions are met with on the way, and this leads to greater social standing. But do not let prudence be overtaken by boastful arrogance.

44 STEM 4 (YIN FIRE) BRANCH VIII
SHEEP LOST ITS WAY

This is an unfavourable moment; resources are exhausted, and it appears that there is no solution to the problem. But a trusted friend will provide help when least expected.

45 STEM 5 (YANG EARTH) BRANCH IX MONKEY OF SELF-RELIANCE

Sometimes it is wise to get away from the crowd and assert your independence. Perhaps this leads to friction and causes enmity; but if it discourages the unwanted attentions of petty acquaintances, so much the better.

46 STEM 6 (YIN EARTH) BRANCH X ROOSTER PECKING FOR SCRAPS

In times of prosperity, make sure that sufficient resources are stored for leaner years. Storms will break even in the height of summer. Look to the ways that present expenditure can be reduced, and the balance transferred to savings.

47 STEM 7 (YANG METAL) BRANCH XI DOG IN THE TEMPLE

The situation is extremely complex, and personalities are difficult to understand. A dilemma causes stress; on one side a feeling of anger seeks vengeful satisfaction, but an inner voice of conscience admits that there are faults on both sides. It is wise to seek a mediator.

48 STEM 8 (YIN METAL) BRANCH XII PIG ON THE FARM

Riches will come from the harvest. Those who deal with vegetables, fruits, herbs and medicines will prosper. A country residence is better than one in the city.

49 STEM 9 (YANG WATER) BRANCH I RAT ON THE MOUNTAIN

No matter how slim the resources, it is possible to lead a full and satisfying life. There is satisfaction at being able to do things without cost that others would have to pay for dearly. Resourcefulness is in itself a virtue.

50 STEM 10 (YIN WATER) BRANCH II OX BY THE GATE

Standing by the door, watching the world go by, this person hears and sees many things. But advice is not given unless it is requested. That is what experience has taught.

51 STEM 1 (YANG WOOD) BRANCH III TIGER STANDING FIRM

The qualities of leadership and management are never so strong as they are at present. With firm determination, it is possible to revitalize a situation that has been allowed to fall into decay. Cut out what is unserviceable and replace it with the new.

52 STEM 2 (YIN WOOD) BRANCH IV RABBIT ATTAINS ENLIGHTENMENT

A mystery is solved at last. The root of the problem is uncovered, so bringing a distressing problem to a most satisfying conclusion. It is time to pause.

53 STEM 3 (YANG FIRE) BRANCH V DRAGON IN THE SKY

The stars of the Dragon constellation shine through the summer night sky in the south direction. It is a propitious omen, promising great success for those following the right course of action.

54 STEM 4 (YIN FIRE) BRANCH VI SNAKE IN THE POOL

The snake cools itself in the water during the heat of summer; there is concealed danger for those who move into unfamiliar surroundings. But those who are content to remain where they are will benefit eventually.

55 STEM 5 (YANG EARTH) BRANCH VII HORSE IN THE STABLE

Sometimes it is better to remain behind instead of trying to catch up with the crowd. This would be advisable, for by staying put danger at home is prevented, while moving would reveal problems in an unfamiliar situation.

56 STEM 6 (YIN EARTH) BRANCH VIII SHEEP IN PASTURE

Progress is steady and proceeds at a gentle pace. The present situation will improve sufficiently to ensure that matters are comfortably managed. Future conditions will be satisfactory.

57 STEM 7 (YANG METAL) BRANCH IX MONKEY EATING FRUIT

Business prospects are highly favourable. The right decisions have been made, and the results are extremely gratifying. Careful management of resources has ensured profitable returns. The outcome is successful.

58 STEM 8 (YIN METAL) BRANCH X ROOSTER IN A CAGE

Conditions are never as satisfactory as they could be. Accept with patience any circumstances that cannot be changed. You will be more content in your new situation.

59 STEM 9 (YANG WATER) BRANCH XI DOG KEEPING WATCH

Being a good judge of character is a valuable asset. It is satisfying to have found the right balance between friendliness and firmness. A reputation for fair dealing is something that cannot be bought.

60 STEM 10 (YIN WATER) BRANCH XII PIG IN THE FOREST

Those who believe that the education of children begins in the home, and that a good family life with moral leadership and example given by the parents is the best gift that a parent can provide, will not only be blessed by former ancestors, but will be respected and revered for many generations to come.

DESCRIPTIVE
NAMES OF STEM-
AND-BRANCH COMBINATIONS

These descriptive names are referred to in the novel *Jin Ping Mei*, written around 1590, but they were certainly known several centuries before that date. In more advanced Chinese astrological calculations, each stem-and-branch pair is combined together to produce a resultant 'Element' – Wood, Fire, Earth, Metal or Water. The descriptive names of the stem-and-branch combinations amplify the individual qualities of these Five Elements, for example, soft wood, hard wood, furnace fire, candle flame and so on. These descriptions of the Elements are not character assessments, but say whether a person will be fortunate or otherwise in life (compare, for example, No. 1 Gold from the Sea with No. 31 Gold from the Mines). It should be noted that there are only 30 descriptive names, with no distinction being made between the Yang and Yin (odd and even) daily numbers.

The descriptive names might be used in conjunction with the stem-and-branch observations in the previous section to determine the outcome of a particular future event, using the same calculation as before.

COMBINED ELEMENTS

Although each stem and Animal Sign has its own Element, the pairing of a stem with an Animal Sign creates a third Element.

STEM-AND-BRANCH PAIRS

1-2 GOLD FROM THE SEA
'Gold from the sea' is treasure washed ashore, or pirate treasure buried in the sand. It signifies that wealth and riches come unexpectedly, without being earned.

3-4 FURNACE FIRE
The furnace is used for smelting gold and precious metals. Those who fashion gold and silver work hard to achieve their riches. Costly resources are not allowed to stand around idly, but are reshaped and made even more valuable.

5-6 FOREST TREE
There are ample resources for achieving the desired results. But it is useless to sit looking at your possessions; those who set to work in earnest and take the lead will continue to gain benefits and add to their resources.

7-8 DITCH EARTH
The earth from the ditch represents the remaining debris of someone else's industry. For those engaged in refuse collection, this is a favourable sign. It can also apply to those dealing in valuable antiques.

9-10 SWORDEDGE METAL
The sword is double-edged; it is impossible to make progress as long as you are tied to the old ways. The decision has to be made to make the final break. This is someone who is prepared for determined and ruthless action.

11-12 BEACON FIRE
The fire on the top of the hill signals news. In bad times, it heralds rejoicing, and in good times, it is advance warning of approaching enemies. Thus it reveals an ability to spot current trends.

13-14 CHANNELLED WATER When water is channelled along a chosen course, it brings great benefits: it transports people and goods and brings wealth; it takes away the dross and restores good health.

15-16 RAMPART EARTH The city boundaries show the limits of protection. It is unwise to stray too far from the present location as there are unknown dangers lurking beyond the walls.

17-18 WHITE METAL There are gains to be had; the prospects are encouraging for those who are realistic and prudent. Far better to achieve a small amount than to lose a great deal.

19-20 SOFTWOOD Although it is easily and quickly worked, softwood is useful only for secondary or temporary structures. There are quick returns but small rewards.

21-22 SPRING WATER The fresh spring refreshes; it is a sign of renewed vigour and recovery from a debilitating illness. It is favourable to take the next step. This is a sign bringing hope and joy to other people.

23-24 ROOFING SLATES Whatever storms may lie ahead, it is reassuring to know that provisions have been made to withstand them. Anything done to secure the future will be well justified.

25-26 LIGHTNING FIRE The lightning signifies inspiration and sudden alteration of circumstances. There is a complete change of direction in life, bringing upheaval and disarray, but those who are well prepared will benefit.

27-28 HARDWOOD Hardwood is a valuable and serviceable material for constructions that are designed to last many years. But much effort is needed to change its form. Valuable resources are put to good use.

29-30 SLOW-FLOWING WATER The river is deep and powerful, but moves sluggishly. There is much to be gained by being careful and patient.

31-32 GOLD FROM THE MINES This is the opposite of 'gold from the sea' in that the wealth will be achieved, but through hard work, rather than by chance.

33-34 FIRE IN THE VALLEY This is the base camp at the foot of a mountain. It is a welcome respite before the arduous climb to the summit. A favourable sign, but the final acclaim comes only after renewed effort.

35-36 SCRUBLAND TWIGS Little can be made with twigs and brushwood but a fire. Great changes can be made by gathering small amounts together into something larger and more beneficial. But the benefits will be short-term.

37-38 EARTHEN WALLS
These provide an adequate defence against foreseen problems in the future; if adequate precautions are taken, no misfortune will come about.

39-40 BRONZE MIRROR
Looking into a mirror is to see into a distant world. It symbolizes the mysteries of Heaven and Earth; divination, astrology and even space travel all fall under the beneficial influences of the bronze mirror.

41-42 CANDLE FLAME
The lamplight provides illumination when the hours are dark. It is a sign of revelation and understanding, and the elucidation of difficulties.

43-44 THE MILKY WAY
The path to the stars shows great ambitions, and the promise of future fame. But idle dreams are not enough. Determination and single-mindedness will unlock the treasures that are there.

45-46 ROADWAY EARTH
There is much to do, and a long way to go. The journey may be arduous, but it will be enjoyable. A willingness to adapt and a lively heart will bring rewards along the way.

47-48 BROOCH PINS
The position in life is comfortable enough to be able to afford jewellery. But personal adornment carries a hidden danger.

49-50 MULBERRY WOOD
The wood of the mulberry tree was used for making charms against disease. It shows recovery from ill health.

51-52 FAST-FLOWING WATER
The water represents communications and travel; the fact that it is fast-flowing signifies a great deal of important correspondence which has to be dealt with urgently. To delay would mean missed opportunities, and problems at a later stage.

53-54 SAND AND CLAY
An unfavourable sign; this sand cannot be used for building, nor is it useful as clay for making pots or bricks. Plans do not bear much fruit.

55-56 HEAVEN FIRE
'Fire from heaven' is lightning and accidental fire; by extension it signifies punishment for wrongdoing. It is vital to be protective of one's person and property.

57-58 POMEGRANATE WOOD
An expensive material for fine works of art; rewards that are of greater worth than their material value. Valuable objects are treasured, bringing contentment and financial gain.

59-60 OCEAN WATER
A long voyage lies ahead; it signifies departure for many years, to live in a distant land, if not through permanent emigration, then for much of one's life.

THE ANIMAL SIGN FOR THE YEAR, MONTH, DAY AND HOUR

THE ANIMAL SIGN
FOR THE HOUR

Up until the beginning of the 20th century, mechanical clocks were a rarity in China. But when a baby was born, it was traditional for the baby's horoscope to be made, and the astrologer would need to know the time of birth. So at the moment of birth, a bystander would light an incense stick. If the baby was born during the night, the incense would be kept burning until dawn, or if it was daytime, until dusk. Then the smouldering stick would be extinguished, and the parents would take the unburnt portion to the fortune-teller. By measuring how much of the incense stick was left, the astrologer would know the hour of birth for the horoscope calculation.

Just as the Animal Signs mark the passage of the seasons of the year, so they mark the passing of time during each day. Each marks a two-hour period: the Rat double-hour being the hours before and after midnight, and the Horse the double-hour that spans midday. The Rabbit reveals the dawn, the Rooster sunset – when the chickens come home to roost!

Finding the Animal Sign for the hour is the easiest part of drawing up a horoscope: the table on page 76, listing the animals for the double-hours, needs no modification.

The facing page gives some suggestions about what to do if the birth time is unknown.

Sometimes there is a query regarding clock time. The time used is local time and usually no modification, other than for Daylight Saving Time if in force, needs to be made. Occasionally there will be borderline cases where adjustments to the hour would need to be made. For example, Brazil, stretching from the Atlantic to the Andes, uses only one time zone, yet Australia, covering a similar difference in longitude, has three. Russia has eleven different time zones, but China, stretching over similar longitudes, has only one. Whether the time of birth is to be adjusted because of locality, or because of Daylight Saving Time depends on a simple rule: when the Sun is at its highest point, it is noon. Remember that the Chinese horoscope is only concerned with two-hour periods, not minutes and seconds, so that the time factor is not usually such a problem.

Another question that gets asked from time to time is what happens when someone is recorded as being born at the exact time between one double-hour and the next, for example at 5.00 am. In such an eventuality it should be assumed that the mid-wife wrote down the time after the baby was born, so that the person's time of birth should belong to the previous double-hour.

IF THE PERSON'S HOUR OF BIRTH IS NOT KNOWN

If the person's time of birth is unknown, use the Rabbit hour if the birth is said to have been in the morning, the Rooster if it is said to have been in the afternoon, or the Rat if it is said to have been at night. If the person has no idea when the birth time was, use the noon hour of the Horse. But remember that the additional sign is only a provisional one. Practised astrologers may feel that a particular Animal

HOURS AND SEASONS

Sunrise, noon, sunset and midnight are the daily equivalent of the four seasons of the year.

Sign ought to be present in the horoscope, but is missing. For example, a person may have a particular quality, perhaps a mischievous nature, that is not revealed by any of the other signs, suggesting that the person was born at the Monkey hour. When the information is missing this will often indicate what the time of birth would have been.

TO FIND THE ANIMAL SIGN FOR THE HOUR

Use the table below to find the Animal Sign for the HOUR of birth. If you don't know the birth time, then, just for practice, use the time it is now. Some remarks on the meaning of this sign will be found on the page listed against each Animal Sign in this table.

WHAT THE ANIMAL OF THE HOUR SIGNIFIES

Just as the month generates the day, so the day generates the hour. It follows that, as the month of birth shows the influences of our parents, the hour represents those over whom we have influence and authority – our children, the younger generation, those who work for us.

The astrological symbolism for each of the Chinese hours derives from the activities of the daily life: thus the hour may reveal further facets of the personality. The following pages show how the Animal Sign for the hour reveals how we perceive, and are perceived by, those over whom we have an influence.

Some astrologers consider that the hour of birth gives an insight into the hidden personality of the individual. Whereas the year sign shows how others perceive the person, the hour sign reveals what the person would secretly like to be. The footballer who wants to be a ballet dancer might have a Horse for the year sign, but a Sheep for the hour sign.

THE DOUBLE-HOURS AND THEIR ANIMAL SIGNS

BIRTH TIME	ANIMAL SIGN	see page	BIRTH TIME	ANIMAL SIGN	see page
23.00–01.00	Rat	78	11.00–13.00	Horse	80
01.00–03.00	Ox	78	13.00–15.00	Sheep	80
03.00–05.00	Tiger	78	15.00–17.00	Monkey	80
05.00–07.00	Rabbit	79	17.00–19.00	Rooster	81
07.00–09.00	Dragon	79	19.00–21.00	Dog	81
09.00–11.00	Snake	79	21.00–23.00	Pig	81

WHEN THE SUBJECT'S HOUR ANIMAL SIGN IS	RELATES FAVOURABLY IF THE DAILY ANIMAL IS	HAS DIFFICULTIES WITH CHILDREN IF THE DAILY ANIMAL IS
RAT 23.00–01.00	Ox, Dragon, Monkey	Horse
OX 01.00–03.00	Rat, Snake, Rooster	Sheep
TIGER 03.00–05.00	Rabbit, Horse, Dog	Monkey
RABBIT 05.00–07.00	Tiger, Sheep, Pig	Rooster
DRAGON 07.00–09.00	Snake, Rat, Monkey	Dog
SNAKE 09.00–11.00	Dragon, Ox, Rooster	Pig
HORSE 11.00–13.00	Sheep, Tiger, Dog	Rat
SHEEP 13.00–15.00	Horse, Rabbit, Pig	Ox
MONKEY 15.00–17.00	Rooster, Rat, Dragon	Tiger
ROOSTER 17.00–19.00	Monkey, Ox, Snake	Rabbit
DOG 19.00–21.00	Pig, Tiger, Horse	Dragon
PIG 21.00–23.00	Dog, Rabbit, Sheep	Snake

As well as revealing a person's inner self, and the way that the subject is likely to interact with the younger generations, the animal for the hour is a useful factor when planning dates for important meetings or events. The year sign is used for lifelong commitments such as marriage; the hour sign is useful for planning the times for meetings or contract signing. If the meeting is to last all day, then a day ruled by an Animal Sign that is compatible with the hour sign will be harmonious. For example, if someone was born at the Rat hour, it would be favourable to have a meeting on a Dragon day.

RAT

23.00–01.00

At midnight most of the household will be asleep; but there will still be some people active at this hour: watchmen are alert, scholars study their books, astronomers gaze at the sky, misers count their hoards. People born at the midnight hour have a disposition to follow nocturnal occupations. To others, these people may seem distant or secretive, but wise.

OX

01.00–03.00

Those born in the darkest hours before the dawn want to reach out to the light. They dislike seeing grim faces and unhappiness around them and try to bring laughter into people's lives. They are fond of making jokes but these are not always appreciated. For this reason, they are seldom taken seriously, which may put them at a disadvantage at critical moments.

TIGER

03.00–05.00

The sky begins to lighten though the Sun has not yet appeared. The early risers prepare for the coming day, to have everything ready before dawn breaks. Such people are always first to take advantage of whatever opportunities arise, and their success is due to alertness rather than luck. Others may regard them as pushy and over-ambitious.

RABBIT

05.00–07.00

At dawn the working day begins, and people go about their daily tasks. Those born at the Rabbit hour are industrious, caring for themselves and their families. They appreciate the advantages of a well-regulated life, and the importance of strong family bonds. They are perceived as caring and responsible.

DRAGON

07.00–09.00

Those who rise late must hurry to get everything finished in time. Instead of tasks being performed with care, they are done in haste, and the results are rarely the better for it. A great deal may be achieved in life, but it would be more satisfactory if everything were to move at a more sedate pace. Employees working under pressure are liable to make mistakes.

SNAKE

09.00–11.00

The morning's work is finished, and it is time to rest and review what needs to be done next. It is satisfying to look back over what has been done, but those who are wisest take time to see whether it could have been done better or more efficiently. Achievement brings contentment, but a desire for continuing improvement may lead to a reputation for being a perfectionist.

HORSE

11.00–13.00

At noon when the Sun is highest, there is much to do out of doors. At work or play, those born at the Horse hour dislike the claustrophobic confines of enclosed spaces. The schoolboy may play truant, the worker may look for occupations in the open air, for either way, there is much to do and much to see in the bigger world outside.

SHEEP

13.00 –15.00

After the midday meal, work begins again. It is time to return to the chores and tasks of the day; not something to be enjoyed, but something that has to be done. Those born during the Sheep hour take their duties seriously, and attend to their responsibilities assiduously. Children or employees may find the constraints of everyday discipline dull and restrictive.

MONKEY

15.00–17.00

The end of the working day approaches, though there is still much to do. Stretching out to ease a creaking back, the worker returns to the job in hand, secure in the knowledge that it will be finished soon. The symbolism shows someone who is beginning to tire of the present situation, and is considering how it might be changed.

ROOSTER

17.00–19.00

Those born at the Rooster hour enter the world at the end of the day, when preparations are being made for the evening meal, and whatever entertainment follows. Their first perception of daily life is one of leisure and pleasure. For the rest of their years they dream of a sybaritic existence in which all their desires are fulfilled.

DOG

19.00–21.00

This is the hour when the city gates are locked, and the night watch goes on duty. It signifies defence and suspicion of strangers. In everyday dealings with people, scepticism and mistrust often become a barrier to understanding and, although not necessarily showing aggression, such people may be regarded as defensive and difficult to know.

PIG

21.00–23.00

The subject of the horoscope was born when everyone was asleep. In quiet, comfortable solitude, the child was reared with care and love, and this peaceful tranquillity is the gift that those born in the Pig hour would most sincerely like to bequeath to those who follow. Healing processes are accelerated with gentle contemplation.

HOW THE ANIMAL SIGNS INFLUENCE EACH OTHER

HARMONY OR DISCORD

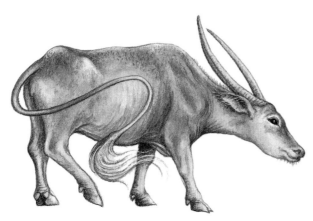

Chinese people who follow the traditional customs pay special attention to the Animal Sign for the birth years of prospective life partners, and there are several proverbs that attest to the likelihood of a marriage's success or failure based on the year signs of the individuals. 'When the Rabbit meets the Snake, there is true happiness', says one.

But the influences of one Animal Sign on another extend to the commercial world. In the Chinese business community, the Animal Signs would be taken into account when considering the wisdom of entering into alliances.

In a more practical way, the harmony or discord that exists between two Animal Signs can be a useful guide to establishing the prospects for a particular day, month or year. When the year Animal is harmonious, it is a time for expansion, a time to loosen the reins, a time to move house or embark on new

ventures. Conversely, when a year Animal opposes the personal Animal Sign, it is a time to take care in business dealings, personal relationships and health matters. In short, a year when it is inadvisable to take risks. Here is a useful guide to the manner in which each Animal Sign has an influence on another. The influencing sign might represent people (such as a prospective partners in personal relationships, business or whatever), or particular periods of time, such as the year, month, day, or even the proposed time of day, for an important event.

These paragraphs describe the influence of external factors, such as the effect other people may have, or whether certain periods of time are likely to prove favourable or not.

The main headings represent the influencing signs, the paragraphs that follow show how those Animal Signs are affected.

LIFE'S PARTNERSHIPS

*More than three thousand years ago, the lyrics of an
anonymous Chinese poet warned that it was folly
for two people to marry if their celestial signs lacked
mutual harmony.*

HOW THE RAT AFFECTS:

ANOTHER RAT

A time for expansion, for getting one's ambitions off the ground, and for deciding to climb up the ladder. The rewards and benefits will be felt later, together with the satisfaction of having made the right decision. There is an abundance of new energy; this should be directed in a positive way, and practical steps taken for the future.

THE OX

With the stimulation brought by the Ox comes upheaval and change. But the cautious Ox sometimes needs to set off in a new direction, and the favourable influence of the Rat can be the spark to light a new ambition. Decisions taken in Rat years may initially be beset with problems but in time, there will be reason to be grateful for having made the right choice.

THE TIGER

A feeling of well-being produces the confidence to look forward to the next stages of development in one's personal life and at work. Consider a change of employment, moving home, or even embarking on the first steps towards a permanent relationship. Health problems can be resolved, and any hidden anxieties can be dealt with satisfactorily.

THE RABBIT

The Rabbit should err on the side of caution. Figuratively, problems will not seem as bad in the morning light, since the Rat represents midnight and the Rabbit the dawn. Use diplomacy and consider the consequences, and irritations caused by petty-minded people will have no place disturbing your tranquillity.

THE DRAGON

The Rat influence is the catalyst that causes you to explode with dynamic enthusiasm. Your magical storehouse of energy runs at full power. If the head of department is a Rat your work will be ambitious and novel. You should make every effort to take advantage of the positive trends that are at work in your favour. It is an ideal time to change jobs, move house, or even embark on a new relationship.

THE SNAKE

The Snake is destined to encounter petty problems, which will be swiftly overcome, but at some loss to the Snake's reputation. In dealing with obstacles, the Snake is likely to seize on any opportunity that seems to prove a means of forestalling an impending difficulty. By acting ruthlessly and without compassion, great advances can be made. But at what cost?

THE HORSE

Being diametrically opposed to the Horse, the Rat has a profoundly malign effect on your ambitions and prospects. The Rat period throws up all kinds of difficulties which could be revealed by government authorities who object to the Horse's plans, or the collapse of contracts, or even the abandonment of plans through the machinations of nature – even something as unpredictable as the weather itself. Avoid any projects that involve water.

THE SHEEP

The Rat has relatively little influence on the Sheep, for the most part helping to continue the earlier happy, positive trends. It is only when the Rat is combined with the Ox in some way (perhaps as a partnership of two people, one being Rat and the other Ox, or else of two time factors) that any unfavourable influence will be felt. When this occurs, the aspect of the Sheep's life that is most likely to be affected lies in the stability or otherwise of its long-term relationship.

THE MONKEY

This is one of the most vibrant periods for the Monkey. You should harness all your renewed energy into ways in which the quality of life can be improved. It is a time to rouse dormant ideas and put them into service. Move swiftly; act on impulse, and take on all contenders. Several opportunities for personal gain are opening up; it is not enough merely to recognize the potential, it is a time for calling on resources and taking action.

THE ROOSTER

Although the Rat and the Rooster do not stand in the best harmonious positions, they are able to support each other in a positive way provided that they do not remain too close. The Rat period therefore brings opportunities with short-term results, but it would be unwise for the Rooster to rely on those remaining as permanent benefits. The Rooster should not take the improved situation for granted; a failure to maintain obligations will soon end the arrangement.

THE DOG

The Rat and the Dog are mutually supportive, although to a limited extent. There will be unexpected help when it is most needed, sometimes financial, sometimes in the guise of valuable advice that can help the Dog to deal with a difficult situation. Positive trends that have emerged in the past will continue to develop and bring benefits.

THE PIG

This is an unsettled time for the Pig. Although new opportunities connected with past experience are offered, there is an instinctive feeling that it could be unwise to make a move into unknown territory. The benefits should be weighed against the disadvantages, as the Rat period is neither a positive nor a negative influence for the Pig. Those with family ties are better remaining in the existing situation; while those who have fewer restrictions and are able to move should take the chance to improve their careers.

HOW THE OX AFFECTS:

THE RAT

The Ox and the Rat are partners in the fields of creativity and production – the Rat beginning and the Ox finishing. The Rat sees the rewards for all its efforts in the past. There will be surprises, some of which can lead to greater security and relief from financial anxiety, while in the area of business and careers comes the satisfaction of seeing long-standing projects brought to a successful conclusion.

ANOTHER OX

The Ox is at its most powerful, intransigent and insurmountable during the Ox year. Those in positions of authority will be reaching the zenith of their careers, and should do their utmost to stabilize their positions. A difficult time lies ahead, but successful negotiations will see the Ox trampling down any opposition.

THE TIGER

It is important to tread cautiously. Normally, the Tiger has no difficulties in facing up to problems, but may now be faced with a new and inexplicable predicament. It is important to ensure that there is good advice and counsel at hand, for the best way to deal with problems at the moment is by diplomacy and tact, weapons with which the Tiger may not be too familiar.

THE RABBIT

This is a period for resolving one's career choices and family commitments. There will be a choice of opportunities: one will bring increased standing and an improved position in society but it will involve changing the home base and moving to a new location. Staying put offers no financial benefits, but brings a happy life, security and greater personal happiness.

THE DRAGON

While the Dragon is fired with enthusiasm and is eager to rush along, the turgid machinations of administrative bureaucracy prevent any apparent progress. But these set-backs are all necessary precautions, as the Dragon will discover. Though reluctant to admit it, the Dragon will be heartily grateful for the delays and obstructions.

THE SNAKE

The Ox brings welcome stability into a somewhat unpredictable age. Of course, the Snake does not want to be permanently tied to a particular base, but at last there seems to be a haven in which to drop anchor during stormy weather. A career opportunity may demand a long-term commitment, and the same is true of a possible future relationship.

THE HORSE

The Horse wants to race; the farmer wants it to pull the plough. For the moment, ambitions have to be laid aside, seemingly trivial matters attended to and all aspects of business life managed thoroughly and efficiently. Before embarking on a journey, make sure your home is secured. There could be trouble in personal relationships. It is useless to try to go in two different directions at once.

THE SHEEP

As a rule, when two Animal Signs are directly opposite each other, they are mutually harmful. But in the case of the Sheep and the Ox it is the humble Sheep who is able to overcome the Ox. Thus, the obstructions that face the Sheep during Ox periods, and which for other Animal Signs would normally prove to be crippling hindrances, actually work in the Sheep's favour. The Sheep may not attain its goal, but it certainly sees that its rivals don't fulfil their ambitions either.

THE MONKEY

Restraints shackle the Monkey's indiscriminate roaming. These may come in many forms: an authoritative figure may warn the Monkey that its talents would find better use at home; at work, scant attention may be paid to what the Monkey regards as its innovative solutions to pressing problems, and travel opportunities may be reduced simply because of the need to budget. Find ways to prune your expenditure, and take time to reassess your everyday needs and requirements.

THE ROOSTER

This is a very favourable period with opportunities to expand in every direction. Where health has been an issue, this too should find some amelioration. Use the ponderous, tradition-oriented influence to your advantage. To be in fashion and style, while others are trying to shock with the ultra-novel, astonish with your interpretation of classic effects. In the commercial world, the longer something lasts, the more attractive it will be.

THE DOG

It is no use shouting and making a fuss; if things aren't going to happen, they won't; the best advice is to rethink your options and to decide on alternative approaches. If the home that you had set your heart on is sold to someone else, or the position you coveted is awarded to a rival, then consider that there are many more opportunities available to someone with your resources and special talents.

THE PIG

This is one of the most favourable times for the Pig. The prevailing influence is one of warmth and happiness, and a general feeling of family togetherness at last fills an emotional gap. There will be opportunities to celebrate, and the genial atmosphere will lead to renewed personal ambitions and a fervent wish to improve your position. Do what you can to make your home life more comfortable and secure and you will have a secure foundation for all your future plans.

HOW THE TIGER AFFECTS:

THE RAT

To the Rat's natural creative gifts are added the Tiger's confidence and authority, giving the Rat the strength to put ideas into practice and realize long-held ambitions. But the Rat has to work for these benefits; they do not come easily. During this positive period, it would be wise not to be too domineering in handling your personal relationships with other people. The Tiger partner is best handled delicately.

THE OX

With continued perseverance, the Ox will eventually succeed. In career matters, it is difficult to avoid confrontation, but you will make your point eventually. In family and partnership matters, take a gentler approach, despite a hostile atmosphere that threatens to make matters worse. Where possible, be tactful. A Tiger partner may be irksome.

ANOTHER TIGER

Establish what you want to achieve, plan your course of action, and proceed. There is much to be gained, but once you have consolidated your position, you can loosen your grip, replacing aggressive action with diplomacy. In your personal relationships, don't let your new self-confidence alienate your partner.

THE RABBIT

Too many distractions are caused by the Rabbit having to spend time trying to patch up differences among friends. In business, trusted methods of making new contacts may not be entirely successful. If you use the low-key approach, make sure that your opposite number knows that the big band is only blowing quietly. In personal relationships, the Rabbit and Tiger partnership works well.

THE DRAGON

There is great excitement in store. Something magical can happen; a project that you thought had no chance of success takes off unexpectedly. Once you have defined your objective, no matter how wild or impractical, a solution can be found. But plans are not enough – they have to be acted on.

THE SNAKE

The Tiger is always suspicious about the Snake's true intentions, while the Snake tends to be intimidated by the Tiger's overt hostility. Consequently, the Snake is going to have to be very careful how it presents itself. If its charm is turned on full power, people will think there is a hidden agenda which the Snake is trying to obscure. It is best to be absolutely honest.

THE HORSE

An invigorating atmosphere of enthusiasm surrounds the Horse at work and at play. This is a wonderful period for extending the circle of business contacts and friends. It is the ideal time for travel to exotic places, and for forging links across continents. Efforts will be amply repaid, and the Horse will look back on this year as the one that marked the start of a new life. For the female Horse who has been unlucky in love, now is your chance to find a partner; but you must make the first move.

THE SHEEP

The Tiger period is the start of a very happy phase for the Sheep. It is a good time for the Sheep to start making plans for large-scale changes: perhaps a house move is foreseen, or a change in marital status. This may well be the year in which these changes take place, although, because of the scale of the changes, the final result may take longer to achieve. The overall spirit of optimism will carry the Sheep along and delays won't matter in the least.

THE MONKEY

The Tiger represents authority in opposition to the Monkey. The Tiger may figure as a senior figure making unreasonable demands that have to be met. A set of unavoidable circumstances or demands may mean that the Monkey's leisure activities have to be curtailed or even abandoned. In personal and business relationships, diametrically opposite views will cause intolerable friction between Monkey and Tiger partners, the Monkey coming out worst.

THE ROOSTER

Traditionally, the Tiger and the Rooster are incompatible, but in the Tiger period the shared qualities of these two self-possessed personalities enhance the Rooster's stamina, powers of expression and general well-being. Thus, the Rooster succeeds much better in its supposedly opposing Tiger year than it does in the year of its own sign. Many opportunities are offered and it is a good time to develop a recently established relationship.

THE DOG

This is a favourable time for the Dog. Others are not only sympathetic and encouraging, but can also assist in practical ways. The Dog's determination and loyalty are rewarded. This is a good time to seek career advancement, and make important changes. This positive period allows the Dog to attend to the important things. With a Tiger partner the Dog will succeed as never before.

THE PIG

The cautious Pig should have gathered in all its winter store by now, as it may be necessary to call upon its resources and savings. This is not the ideal time for making great changes; career moves are likely to bring the Pig into conflict with senior management, and a new position may not fulfil the expectations that seemed so attractive. Make the best of the situation and see what future improvements can be planned. Towards the end of the year be prepared for further calls on your resources, but the purpose will ultimately be beneficial.

HOW THE RABBIT AFFECTS:

THE RAT

Although many of the events of the year are noteworthy at the time, few of them will last long in the memory. Do not plan to make great changes, as circumstances may conspire to rearrange your priorities. Long-established links may be broken, and you may find that former friends have made plans of their own in which you assumed, wrongly, you would be included.

THE OX

You may surprise everyone by becoming more outward looking and less resistant to change. You can throw off the shackles of convention, and adopt a more positive attitude. A fresh approach to dealing with complex situations will improve career and business prospects, while a closer understanding of the way other people choose to lead their lives will cement closer family relationships.

THE TIGER

This period is when the aggressive Tiger borrows the Rabbit's wisdom on making friends and influencing people, discovering that charm and compliance can often be more impressive than an unequivocal demand. In your personal life, events will help you adjust your values and perceptions of people.

ANOTHER RABBIT

Do not put your priorities to one side in favour of perceived commitments and obligations to others, but decide for yourself what your prime objectives are, and aim for them. For once, you have a chance to be the leader rather than the follower. Do not be satisfied with what is on offer, but demand alternatives.

In personal relationships and family life, this could be a golden period. Cherish it.

THE DRAGON

Financially, this is a most unfavourable time for the Dragon who likes to take risks. In all commercial undertakings, this is a time for extreme caution. Even the soundest foundations are likely to be cracked. But if you keep to a steady, humdrum path, resources will be preserved for more favourable opportunities later. Personal relationships are exciting.

THE SNAKE

A proverb says that when 'the Snake and Rabbit meet, there is true happiness'. This augurs well for the Snake in the Rabbit year, with the promise of ambitions being realized, and true love found at last. In business and career, it shows the promise of a position that will bring job satisfaction or financial reward.

THE HORSE

Many of the Horse's ambitious projects will have to be put on hold for the moment. This is the wrong time to try to better yourself. Nothing substantial will be gained, and the Horse might well feel that the time could have been more satisfactorily spent elsewhere. Conditions are not wholly adverse, however, and with patience, and reduced expectations, the Horse person can enjoy what the passage of time brings. Perhaps it is more of a time for friends and more intimate relationships.

THE SHEEP

This year could be a highlight in the life of the Sheep. Career and business matters run smoothly, but in personal relationships it is time to take the plunge, throw off the old persona and adopt a new lifestyle. This can lead to interesting developments in your social life which will improve business contacts and career prospects. But while you are casting off the old and taking on the new, you may be surprised and disappointed to find that other links break off too.

THE MONKEY

Minor changes will affect the Monkey personality. It will need all its manipulative skills to deal with the constant comings and goings of the people in its everyday life. At work there will be changes, and the spotlight on certain events will demand quick thinking. Additions to the family will require ingenuity, while home life could be complicated. The key word during this period is circumspection.

THE ROOSTER

This could be one of the happiest times in the Rooster's life, with wonderful new opportunities promising a brighter future. Sadly, however, there are many factors that conspire to bring this idyllic existence to an end, yet the events of the year will remain happy memories for a long time to come. Business is mixed with pleasure, but during the present eccentric phase it is important to keep the two sides of your life apart.

THE DOG

The usual everyday problems at home and in your family life are enough to cope with for the moment, and it may not be wise to try to embark on anything that is going to make great demands on what little time is left. Attend to small matters; ensure that everything is done to rectify a situation the moment a problem arises and ensure that there are no loose ends. All that done, home and family life should be contentedly replete.

THE PIG

Great happiness awaits the Pig. Home life seems more comfortable and assured, with the advent of young footsteps into the household. At work, there is harmony between staff at all levels, and commercial ventures prosper. You can think about new ventures, and consider furthering your career and improving your home situation. Prospects for distant travel are clearly indicated, with the promise of relocation to another country, but it is not the ideal time to make such a move.

HOW THE DRAGON AFFECTS:

THE RAT

Plans that may have been many years in the making at last come to fruition. There is financial reward, both deserved and unexpected. Business matters that seemed at a standstill suddenly come to life. Seize this new development, using the new prosperity to build a solid future.

THE OX

The patience of the Ox is tested to the limit. When all the trappings of digital technology are unloaded on to the unwilling shoulders of the traditionalist Ox, it can't wait for the moment to say 'I told you so.' It is only when the Ox is eventually convinced of the advantages of the new system that it begins to go wrong. Nothing is satisfactory this year.

THE TIGER

The Tiger's ambitions have the promise of being fulfilled. When a vacant place arises because someone moves to another location, be ready to pounce. The opportunities are there for the taking, but not for long. Delay will bring disappointment. However, having achieved the initial success, do not strive to expand still further, since it may be difficult to maintain your hold. It is more important to consolidate.

THE RABBIT

The Rabbit will succeed during this turbulent period through diligent effort and consideration for the welfare of others. There will be many curious coincidences and other signs that suggest that mysterious forces are at work. Career prospects are steady, while personal relationships continue to bump along the usual puzzling path.

ANOTHER DRAGON

For the lion-tamer, aspiring magician or opera star, this is a wonderfully productive time. But for less exotic Dragons there is a stimulus to release some of those hidden yearnings to throw off social conventions and do something really extraordinary for once. By all means take the chance. In brief, a time to be rash and bold.

THE SNAKE

Although perhaps not as radically adventurous as the Dragon, the Snake personality cannot help but be caught up in its magical influence. The Snake involved in any kind of research may unexpectedly stumble on helpful clues to the subject of the investigation. In the area of career advancement, be aware that vital information that would help your advancement may lie at your fingertips. Follow your hunches.

THE HORSE

The sporting Horse will benefit from a number of minor gains during this eventful period. While luck may be a significant factor, the more skilful the players, the luckier they become. In general, this is a favourable time for the Horse, with several opportunities for self-improvement. But once it is felt that the positive influence is beginning to wane, don't expect it to return. It is a sign that it is time to return to hard-headed logic once again.

THE SHEEP

The Dragon likes to add a touch of magic to most people's lives, but the Sheep has every reason to be wary of these strange influences. The Sheep may resent having to come to terms with new methods of working or plans for modernization that it mistrusts. The solution is to make your misgivings known very clearly, but to cooperate with a show of reluctant willingness. Time may prove you right.

THE MONKEY

When the Dragon and Monkey combine forces, it is bad news for everyone else. In commercial activities, business rivals have every reason to be apprehensive. In career moves, the way to the top may be an unconventional one. Take care not to stretch the bounds of accepted convention too far. In matters of health, accidents are likely to be the result of your own folly, but recovery will be speedy. In your personal life, a new romantic attachment may not be a permanent one, but this will not dampen your natural exuberance.

THE ROOSTER

This is a time of spectacular successes and disheartening disappointments for the Rooster person. Yet it is far from being a disastrous year; the low points are only perceived as such because of the heady peaks that have also been reached. Kissing three frogs and finding only two princes is not a failure. Career prospects follow an uneven path; it would be advisable to adopt a more traditional approach to your projects in future. In personal relationships, remember the remark about the three frogs.

THE DOG

The Dog is well-advised to keep well clear of any get-rich-quick schemes. Fortunately, you are sufficiently in touch with reality to distinguish the false from the genuine. Be suspicious of offers that appear to be too beneficial. In business matters, the same cautious prudence is wise. Perhaps not a year for raising one's hopes, although the spirit of pessimism should be temporary. Personal relationships may not favour the Dog this year.

THE PIG

For the Pig, the advent of the Dragon year is often a matter of overwhelming indifference. The influences are neither favourable nor unfavourable when compared with the havoc and upheaval that affects the people all around you. It is fortunate that you can remain a wry observer of the dramas and extraordinary events that unfold in the lives of your nearest and dearest, chuckling at the thought of the lucky escape you've had.

HOW THE SNAKE AFFECTS:

THE RAT

It often proves to be a fractious year, with the Rat facing problems from unforeseeable quarters: so-called friends prove not to be so; in the workplace treachery and backbiting may halt your hopes of advancement. But you should be able to turn all your misfortunes to a good end. You have an opportunity to reframe your life, and change direction.

THE OX

Favourable influences help you to climb the career ladder, while there are improved prospects for personal relationships. This is an excellent time to change jobs, particularly if this means relocating. The most marked influences are in business, which show success if you run your own concern. Slow progress in any legal processes will soon be resolved.

THE TIGER

You are unable to deal personally and tangibly with problems as they arise, and important matters have to be laid in the hands of a third party, leaving you feeling frustrated and isolated. It is important to choose trustworthy advisers, and allow the burden to rest on them. You have to contend with underhand dealing at every turn.

THE RABBIT

Personal relationships will reach a high point, bringing joy and satisfaction, even though friends may affect to be shocked. If you are circumspect and able to maintain a realistic view of the situation, these can be memorable times. After this, finance and career may not seem important. Watch the budget carefully.

THE DRAGON

Although it will be some time before ambitious plans can be given the starting signal, there is no reason why this stimulating period should not be used in as constructive a way as possible. There are letters to be written, contacts to be made, and potential backers to be won over. Business and career prospects show promise, and your personal relationships have the ingredients for your future happiness.

ANOTHER SNAKE

In all spheres of life there are positive opportunities that should not be allowed to pass by. Personal advancement and public recognition of your achievements will be priorities. There will be invitations to society events and introductions to influential people. Researchers and those with links to the legal profession are favoured.

THE HORSE

There may be too much emphasis on leisure, and not enough on hard work, for the Horse to make this a memorably productive year, but there will be no shortage of memorable events, some of which may be recalled later with an unenviable frisson of discomfiture. The best advice is to take life easy, without getting involved too readily in adventures that put both limb and reputation at risk.

THE SHEEP

You may have been content and happy, yet feeling there was something missing. You can now be more adventurous, and perhaps move from the cloistered confines of the family circle. A new career, or else a change of location is very possible. Both these examples are indicative of the major changes that could come into effect. Interesting news leads to a regular correspondence. There are mild, but permanent adjustments to your life, bringing greater satisfaction.

THE MONKEY

There are so many things that you want to do, and so many ways for your ambitions to be thwarted. The Snake period represents the Monkey struggling with paperwork, and continually burgeoning regulations that restrict its creative freedom. Perhaps it would be as well to seek another's opinion – it often happens that trying to demolish someone else's argument reveals the flaws in your own. It is a difficult period for personal relationships, which may need time to cool.

THE ROOSTER

This is a very special time for personal relationships, and it may be that business and personal life can at last be linked. Strong partnerships are indicated, which leads to improved career prospects, the widening of the social circle and publicity of the most favourable kind. Ambitions are realized, and the Rooster with close family ties will have just cause to be proud of younger members.

THE DOG

You should endeavour to be totally self-reliant. Delays when something needs to be done quickly will inevitably be the fault of other people lacking any sense of urgency. Reliability is hard to find during this frustrating period, and to guard against these minor irritations it would be wise to have more than one solution to any problem. Instil the spirit of competition. Whether at work or in the family, a determined attitude and a few well-chosen plain truths plainly spoken may not go amiss.

THE PIG

The Pig, which usually symbolizes comfort and rest, is in for a rude awakening this year. Several events conspire to interrupt the normal course of events in everyday life. Illness may contribute to the cancellation of plans made long in advance. Another factor that needs to be monitored is the arrival of adult newcomers to the household who may not share your views and ideals, and may be an uncomfortable presence. In the workplace, don't take on more responsibility than you can manage.

HOW THE HORSE AFFECTS:

THE RAT

Just when you seem to be reaching a peak, a major incident upsets your security and happiness. Take the utmost care, not only in business and career matters but also in your personal life. This is an inauspicious time to move house. You will suffer from allergies and sun-related complaints.

THE OX

Many seem to have plenty of spirit to further their own ends, but are unwilling to offer help to someone they perceive as a threat. When drive and enthusiasm are needed, you will get encouragement from an unlikely source. Pursue what you feel to be the right course; success will follow. In personal relationships, a lack of understanding reveals secrets.

THE TIGER

This very vital period will see the career Tiger advancing rapidly, in sure line for promotion. In commercial transactions, you will receive benefits additional to those expected. Home improvements will bring greater comfort and satisfaction than had been visualized. Long-distance travelling will be substantially rewarding. Tigers still looking for a partner have a good chance of success.

THE RABBIT

With all the extra commitments at work and in family life it will be impossible to sit back and dream. But despite the constant bustle of everyday life, the Rabbit will still retain its happy composure. The rest of the world is not indifferent to the sheer determination of the Rabbit, and its dedication and service will eventually be recognized.

THE DRAGON

Two of the Dragon's favourite activities – its career and its social life – take a great bite out of its calendar. It is of course essential that the Dragon does not overreach itself, and ensure that ample space is left for recuperation. Nevertheless, all the hectic activity does not lead to a permanent position, since most of the events of the year are transitory.

THE SNAKE

For Snakes, this is an ideal time to strike, to snatch the opportunity that appears so unexpectedly. In business mildly favourable transactions are turned to great advantage. In career matters, renewed self-assurance brings the confidence to promote yourself. Personal relationships take on a new dimension, causing some envy in your social circle.

ANOTHER HORSE

The Horse's own sign now exerts its strongest influence. Since the Horse itself represents the Yang force, during the times of maximum Yang (the Horse year, mid-summer, and midday) the Horse becomes too confident, and overvalues the contributions – physical assistance, finance, or even affection – it is inclined to make. As it is impossible to take the offerings without the Horse, it is often the case that the Horse may have to be turned away.

THE SHEEP

This is a beneficial year. An invigorating atmosphere gives you enthusiasm and determination. There are many ambitions that have been left unfulfilled; this could be the perfect moment to realize dreams and ambitions. Careers are well favoured. Commercial ventures fare well, and it is a good time for those considering travelling or changing direction. Romantic partnerships formed during this period will be long-lasting.

THE MONKEY

The Monkey may make plans for the future with qualified assurance: something tangible has to be done while the chances are available. Unless acted on now, plans will always remain just that for the present positive phase and the available opportunities are not going to last for ever. That cautionary remark having been made, for the determined Monkey person there is much to be gained. Everything depends on an accumulation of a number of minor matters coming together at the right time.

THE ROOSTER

To avoid the present period's enterprises becoming swamped with controversy and dissent, avoid being drawn into any challenge to your authority. This is a time for the Rooster person to use diplomacy. What is left unsaid, or even undone, can be used as ammunition later. The Rooster faces problems in several different areas. Fortunately, there are people who can carry some of the burden caused by having to be in several places at once. A new friendship may become deeper and more significant.

THE DOG

Periods ruled by the Horse bring causes for celebration. The Dog who is keen on sporting and competitive activities will have many achievements. Those hoping to move house will find an idyllic but invigorating location. In business and commercial activities, progress is very satisfactory. Again, while family life is a just reason for pride, it is mainly in the field of self-advancement that the Horse year's influence is most noticeable.

THE PIG

While the Horse year is an active time for most people, it does not affect you so markedly. There is much that you have to achieve by your own efforts and additional responsibilities would be too distracting. While little seems to be achieved tangibly, there is much to be completed before the big event. Getting the ground prepared takes time. The favourable aspect is that you are relieved and satisfied to find that everything is going to plan.

HOW THE SHEEP AFFECTS:

THE RAT

This is a conciliatory time for the Rat. Major incidents in the past adversely affected your career and health. The time has come to start anew; it may be a struggle to move forward but eventually the peaks will be reached, and there are even greater heights to be achieved. Despite the prevailing circumstances of the moment, look forward with confidence.

THE OX

Beware seemingly innocent remarks, or wonderful offers that cannot be refused. In business, do not take everyone's loyalty for granted; in your personal life, beware treacherous friends; where home, health and car are involved, make sure that your insurance is adequate. If you proceed with caution, you can succeed where others have failed.

THE TIGER

It will be the apparently insignificant events that will loom alarmingly unless they are all attended to and despatched with alacrity. Ignoring minor problems will see them burgeoning, rather than dwindling. If you act with prudence you will have no cause for alarm. Opportunities for self-advancement should not be taken up at the moment.

THE RABBIT

This is a good time to embark on a new career stage. In business and career, there could be an entirely different change of direction, such as from a science- or technology-based occupation to one more connected with the arts. A financially rewarding period, giving greater scope for leisure activities. Enjoyment of family life is enhanced. In your personal life a romantic quality is very uplifting.

THE DRAGON

In the latter part of the year demands will be made on financial resources; there are strong indications that it will be necessary to help in a family emergency, or a close family member may need assistance in moving to a new home. If a promise of engagement or business in a foreign country looms, don't be too optimistic.

THE SNAKE

A touch of cynicism will be a valuable asset when looking over any proposals. The outcome can be substantially favourable, but during the initial stages, optimism should be tempered with scepticism. Looking at plans in a realistic light can avoid disappointment. Otherwise, business and career proceed satisfactorily. Home and family bring contentment.

THE HORSE

Personal relationships take on a new importance. The unattached career-minded Horse may be alarmed to be reminded of its responsibilities and liabilities. The Horse who has been seeking a life partner can find happiness in this eventful period. The time is propitious, and apart from the fact that personal life will intrude in business and career matters, this is a time for celebration.

ANOTHER SHEEP

A time of energy and expansion. Power and authority is now vested in the Sheep, and no matter how insurmountable the obstacles may have seemed in the past, the most fearsome idols can be seen to be no more than images of clay. Do not fear to make your views known; you will be surprised to find how support rallies round you to dismantle the opposition. In business and career, the moment has come to be venturesome. In your personal life you must be absolutely clear about what it is you want from a relationship.

THE MONKEY

The Monkey may find itself left to its own devices. Life may seem to lack excitement and challenge, and there is a danger that you may become dissatisfied and take unwarranted risks. It is wiser to stay put. Any abrupt or ill-considered changes would see resources pointlessly depleted. Patience is needed, and the best way to deal with the situation is to ensure that time is used valuably. Personal relationships are likely to be very strained.

THE ROOSTER

One would not expect the Sheep period, with its implicit gregarious affability, to be one that would exert a benign effect on the maverick Rooster, but you will mellow to achieve your personal ends. This newly discovered side to your character will win friends, leading you to fresh opportunities in business and career. But you cannot maintain this facade for long. There are good prospects, nevertheless, for your personal relationships.

THE DOG

While the Dog can get on with its own life during the Sheep period, there are many interruptions, and some of these will be so distracting that they may cause you to lose sight of your target. Other people are time-consuming. The outcome will be good if problems are dealt with diligently. In your personal relationships, you may feel pulled in two directions, unable to decide what your priorities are.

THE PIG

Lots of welcome news during the Sheep year makes this one of the happiest and most successful periods for Pigs. You can reach your targets through hard work. You will see that no time is wasted in your determination to gain the maximum benefit from the present opportunities. There is so much to be gained, and the result will see you far more comfortably placed than could have been anticipated. In family and home life too there are some joyous occasions in store.

HOW THE MONKEY AFFECTS:

THE RAT

The prospects begin to look highly favourable, and the foundations are laid for future success. Career prospects blossom, and for the Rat engaged in creative work, its achievements begin to be recognized. Many valuable contacts will be made. After the initial rejoicing, there will be a few setbacks but there are greater things in store. In personal relationships, there are favourable developments.

THE OX

The Ox has very strong views, and will be irritated by suggestions that some of its views do not tally with current thinking. Time will prove the Ox to have had the better judgement. There will be setbacks due to technological malfunction. In personal relationships, the Ox is likely to tire of a younger partner's manners.

THE TIGER

The Tiger has failed to take into account that this is an imperfect world. People are limited and can be in only one place at a time. In an emergency the Tiger is likely to find telephone lines continually engaged, and services occupied with other callers. But the Tiger is an autocrat; self-reliance is even more important during this stressful period.

THE RABBIT

While there are moments of comedy during the vexatious rule of the Monkey to brighten the humdrum of everyday life, the same levity becomes irksome when uncurtailed. Such intrusions should not be allowed to affect your relationships with friends or family. Often, the need for loyalty and confidentiality makes it difficult to turn to friends for help. This negative phase is only temporary, fortunately.

THE DRAGON

This is a wonderful time for personal development, for setting out on new adventures and for celebrating. A break with the past lifts a burden from your shoulders. Travel with an exotic companion is foreseen, but watch your financial resources carefully.

THE SNAKE

Instead of being able to get on with important personal matters, unwanted friends or technological breakdown at home or in communications cause disruption. In personal relationships, problems may be caused by misunderstandings, so don't get too closely involved with someone who does not speak the same language. Business and career move forward, but it is not a smooth run.

THE HORSE

Business and commercial dealings plod along, and while finances may not be greatly improved, there is no need for anxiety. Much more important is the greater feeling of satisfaction in all walks of life. Home circumstances are comfortably settled. New friendships lead to fresh leisure interests, which, in turn, lead to even more friendships. This period produces renewed vigour and physical well-being.

THE SHEEP

The positive emphasis is on the arts, and Sheep who are fond of music, reading and fine art will find this an intellectually enriching period. For the others, it will not be enough to follow the crowd; it is important to try to assert your individuality. One way of doing this, which would bring unexpected future benefits, would be to try to master a manual skill.

ANOTHER MONKEY

What excitement lies ahead for the Monkey when the wheel of fortune turns full circle. This is the moment to hoist the anchor and set sail for new shores, no matter how rickety the vessel. Ingenuity and skill will help the Monkey to cope with a whole cargo of quandaries, and though the ultimate destination may be uncharted, the final port will bring rich returns. In all walks of life, the Monkey stands to gain, but only after considerable effort and with a readiness to be flexible. The Monkey's personal life will be full of adventure; some relationships may become too close.

THE ROOSTER

The beginning of a friendship draws the Monkey to the Rooster, but eventually it becomes a tiresome bond. During years ruled by the Monkey, you are likely to become the focus of attention which is flattering, but eventually tedious. Social activities must not be allowed to intrude too heavily on your personal or business life. There is need for an escape hatch, and the invention of a fictitious aunt who requires urgent assistance from time to time is a useful ploy to have in reserve.

THE DOG

There is much to enjoy in life, but you tend to get too easily distracted from the more serious business of the time. Be careful in your daily affairs, and don't place important matters in inexperienced hands. When you have to delegate, ensure that the work is constantly supervised. No matter how desirable it would be to get away from the home base, it is important to be on call at all times. That being so, you can enjoy the fulfilment of an eventful personal relationship.

THE PIG

If you have never done a spot of gardening, now is the time to start. Even if you don't have a garden, you should find friends who would welcome help cultivating their own plots. This is not the best of times to stay indoors in a closed environment. Getting involved in outdoor activities will help during this period. Vary your activities – do not allow yourself to be tied to a repetitious routine.

HOW THE ROOSTER AFFECTS:

THE RAT

Despite the glittering opportunities that seem to be in profusion, there are often concealed dangers and the probable consequences of any actions should be balanced against the alternative solutions. Roosters exert a kind of fascination for you, but though a relationship may be long-lasting, you may suffer anxieties and heartache because of their intransigence.

THE OX

You can indulge your creative fantasies and put some of your ideas into practice without having to worry about other people's opinions. If you are involved in manufacturing or trade this is a very prosperous period. For the career-minded, there are higher positions, if you can adjust your working methods. In personal relationships, happiness is no longer elusive.

THE TIGER

There will be many challenges from those whom you respect but are unwilling to serve. A source of conflict will be solved by a division rather than a sharing of responsibilities. This could leave you with reduced resources, but plenty of space in which to expand. Though this might appear to be taking a step backwards, the outcome will be favourable.

THE RABBIT

Be prepared for setbacks and disappointments. It is not a favourable time to begin new commercial ventures, or look for new premises. A family member disrupts the harmony of the home with unacceptable behaviour. Confrontations are likely to be augmented with threats, but you should stand your ground, no matter what, as you will be the victor.

THE DRAGON

You may find that your best ideas have been stolen and used to benefit someone else, so that you will have missed the rewards that were rightfully yours. Great care should be taken in dealing with others, especially when they take too keen an interest in your work. In personal relationships, a trusted acquaintance may have motives that are potentially hurtful.

THE SNAKE

As the Snake comes to life in the sunshine, this signifies a very favourable period, particularly for the career-minded. Encouragement for your work comes from an unexpected source, and the resulting social contacts lead to fresh opportunities to further your ambitions. During this busy and vital period you should consider all options and seize the moment.

THE HORSE

Rising prices affect your plans, not only as far as business is concerned, but also for your expectations of leisure. It is infuriating to have to forego things that are not absolutely necessary, but common sense prevails. By reducing expenditure, you can enjoy less ostentatious pleasures that will bring just as much satisfaction. Don't be extravagant in your personal relationships.

THE SHEEP

The months of rehearsal and practice, of anticipation and anxiety, will now repay all that effort, patience and stamina. It is time to claim the honour that is your due. At work, there is quiet satisfaction, knowing that you have achieved your aim. In the family, there is pride and sadness as someone close embarks on a new life. You have many choices, but whichever one is taken will bring happiness.

THE MONKEY

When the Rooster and the Monkey both represent people, the symbolism signifies two persons with the same objectives, but two different ways to achieve them. In striving to achieve your ambition, you are impeded at every stage by circumstances dictating the way in which you must act, like someone standing watching over your shoulder, giving advice that is neither solicited nor welcome, nor even accurate. A frustrating time at work may lead you to consider alternative employment. It is better to wait. Family and friends fail to grasp why you give certain matters priority.

ANOTHER ROOSTER

Rooster on Rooster is one of the few exceptions to the general rule that an Animal Sign prospers during its own sign period. In ancient Chinese, this sign was represented by a wine bottle, which figuratively could mean wine or medicine. The double Rooster indicates dependence on medicines, or worse, recreational drugs. It would be far better to alleviate the stress you are experiencing by spending a period of time away from your usual home base or place of work.

THE DOG

A time of peaks and troughs, mountains and valleys, and a real rollercoaster ride as you hurtle from joy to despair. Travel is likely to be cut short abruptly to resolve some domestic disaster, only for you to be hauled off equally abruptly to attend to important business that cannot be postponed. It is best not to make any plans this year. Personal relationships would be good if you could hold on to them.

THE PIG

There will be cause for pride in several aspects of life. For a while, the home will be the centre of activity as joyful news brings delight and celebration. A vigorous atmosphere in the workplace surrounds you and your companions and colleagues as you are drawn into a novel and exciting venture, though one connected only indirectly with the business itself. In personal life there may be a few moments to snatch the beginning of a romance – if you can find the time.

HOW THE DOG AFFECTS:

THE RAT

The Dog defends you against intrusive events that could upset your stability. Only in the matter of personal relationships is the Dog's loyalty divided. Just as domestic dogs always retain their fidelity to their first owners, so it is that if you have a troubled personal relationship in a Dog period, it can be frustrating to discover that there seems to be more sympathy for your partner.

THE OX

Although problems are inevitable, perseverance will eventually prove the best course of action. Setbacks are likely to come from unexpected problems regarding the construction of the home or business premises. A relationship may go sour because of a failure by both partners to see the other's point of view.

THE TIGER

You do not always have the resources to pursue your grander ambitions. But this year brings the right people together in the right place and at the right time, with the potential for great success, and many dreams that were laid to one side may now be fulfilled. In home and family life, there is much to be enjoyed, and personal relationships become closer.

THE RABBIT

It is not a time to embark on any major modifications to your usual routine, and you should only move home or change your career if obliged to do so by circumstances. It is important to avoid accidents, and to keep away from unhealthy environments. Personal relationships are more likely to be irksome than pleasurable. Time will heal all wounds.

THE DRAGON

A disability or illness may contribute to reduced self-esteem. Fortunately, this phase is only temporary, and after a suitable period of rest it will not be long before you regain your famous charisma. Work plods along, but needs your stimulation to produce style and enthusiasm. Personal relationships may lose some magic, but don't worry unduly about this.

THE SNAKE

You will have difficulty trying to make your point of view understood and a suspicion that you are not being entirely truthful can make progress in every sphere of life arduous. The reasons are not clear – they may be the result of rumours laid by a rival. The Snake is adept at getting to the roots of such situations, and this would be a good time to hone these skills.

THE HORSE

The Dog and Horse share many common interests, and in the Dog year you can be sure of encouragement and support. The atmosphere is charged with excitement and optimism. Prospects at work are improved; competition is friendly and open, and the cause of a former unpleasant situation is at last removed, giving you a free rein. Personal relationships hold the promise of permanence.

THE SHEEP

It would be advisable to avoid important interviews on a day ruled by the Dog as the results of any discussion could place you in a subservient position or a post inferior to your present one. This adverse situation passes eventually, but for the moment it is best to follow the prevailing trends. The same is true of partnerships and personal relationships which tend to be wearisome at the present time.

THE MONKEY

Contacts with friends bring some curious changes in plans and the end of the year will not be what was anticipated in the earlier months. Such changes in plans will be entirely discretionary, and the Monkey personality is likely to take up the challenges not so much for personal gain as for the novelty and opportunity to diversify and gain experience. Business plans or career prospects can be said to be neither favourable nor unfavourable, but will provide more interesting developments at a later stage. Personal relationships will go through a wayward phase.

THE ROOSTER

This is a much more favourable period for the stay-at-home Rooster than for the one who is ambitious and seeks an opportunity for career advancement. Setbacks and disappointments may make you feel disheartened, but this is simply because things are not going as perfectly as the fastidious Rooster would like. Be realistic and prune ambitious plans accordingly. Romance and successful business deals can be achieved if these two aspects of life are kept distinctly separate.

ANOTHER DOG

The Dog's own year is a vitally crucial time for anyone born under its sign. Any plans concerning the home, whether alterations or extensions to the house, or even moving house altogether, can be begun with confidence this year. In the workplace, there are positive changes, and the career-minded Dog should decide on its next role. In personal matters, you should make an existing relationship official.

THE PIG

Although you normally favour close ties to home and family, this year a spirit of rebellion may stimulate the urge to set off on some adventure. If ever you wanted to astonish, this is the time when it will succeed. At work, you will be more assertive and demand greater responsibility. Those engaged in merchandizing can expand their product range. Young or old, the Pig personality takes on a subtle change this year, enjoying the company of a partner from an altogether different walk of life.

HOW THE PIG AFFECTS:

THE RAT

This is a period of waiting, so the time should be used for routine everyday affairs, rather than attempting to start fresh ventures when it is not propitious. Rather than trying to leap on to a boat coming in to dock, why not wait in the harbour for the next sailing?

THE OX

Some career openings are offered; they have to be weighed against the fact that the existing situation is already showing improvement. A contented life does not need to be changed. In family matters, there is certainly great satisfaction to be had in the way that matters are developing, and personal relationships too are generating greater empathy.

THE TIGER

There are so many things to be done to further career prospects that having to attend to family and other domestic matters can be more than just a nuisance. However, the opportunities presenting themselves are not singular events. By holding back, you will be able to take advantage of even better offers. Domestic matters take the upper hand. Personal relationships should be kept separate from business ones.

THE RABBIT

In the Pig year the Rabbit's secret ambitions are realized, and its hopes fulfilled. Those employed in the caring, medical or teaching professions will be raised to a higher position, while those in business and commerce will receive honours for their charitable work. A successful period for expansion, and the ideal time to move house. Relationships are very amenable.

THE DRAGON

The Dragon living away from home may be racked by homesickness, leading to a lack of concentration. But this mood will also overtake the Dragon living within the claustrophobic confines of a large household. There will be an urge to travel. This is not the most favourable time for any irreversible changes, so plans will have to be laid very carefully.

THE SNAKE

With the sign of the Pig ruling, the fortunes of the Snake are at their nadir; life can only get better. It is far better to respect the opinions of others than try to change them, far better to know you are right than to be proven wrong. Your patience during this period will be well rewarded, and your tolerance will be remembered at a later date.

THE HORSE

When there is no support from home for your ambitions, and a singular lack of enthusiasm from family, you find yourself alone and needing to fend for yourself. This should be regarded positively, for you gain a great deal of valuable experience, and will realize the true value of taking sole responsibility for your decisions and actions. Personal relationships may founder, but this will be beneficial.

THE SHEEP

Organizational skills are in demand, and those who have the ability to organize festivals, conferences and other events on a grand scale will find this year very profitable and rewarding. For Sheep people generally, the year promises great success in career and commercial ventures. In the matter of personal relationships, this is a time when emergent partnerships can establish a permanent basis.

THE MONKEY

Take advice from older and more experienced colleagues or family friends. This is something that you will find tiresome if not almost impossible to do, but it will be worth the effort. In trying to achieve far too much, the danger is that a great deal will be left unfinished. In some aspects of business there are financial gains to be made, but the challenge is to find the specific areas where your versatility and acumen will be of the greatest assistance, and this is where it needs a trusted opinion. There are some unexpected developments in your personal life.

THE ROOSTER

After going through a difficult time, the influence of the Pig on the Rooster is mildly favourable, and a feeling of renewed confidence brings greater self-esteem. This will lead to improvement in personal relationships. There are closer family ties, with old quarrels being patched up. Generally, a sense of inner satisfaction predominates during this quietly positive phase.

THE DOG

While this may be a good opportunity to take a step back and review your ambitions, there is danger that the prevailing relaxed atmosphere makes you too complacent and you may wake up to find that you have been overtaken by your slower competitor. In the workplace, it may no longer be necessary to be the driving force, but you should keep a lookout for potential problems. In emotional and personal relationships, a gentle approach brings a favourable response.

ANOTHER PIG

Although this is your own year, it is less a time for action than a period for enjoying the rewards of an industrious and well-organized life. The pleasures of the moment are in the enjoyment of past accomplishments, and the satisfaction of creating delightful memories that will last a lifetime. This gently rolling period of grace will give you the time to revitalize and restore your energies, ready for a fresh assault on the world and able to overcome all obstacles. But not just yet.

4

PATTERNS OF HARMONY

THE **FOUR TRIANGLES**

A combination of three or four of the Animal Signs reveals many interesting details. One of the most important is the Four Triangles.

The 12 Animals can be arranged into four sets of three signs which combine harmoniously together. These are the *San Ho*, or Triple Harmonies, and they occur when an Animal Sign is combined with both of its ideal partnerships, which in the case of, for example, the Dragon, would be the Rat and the Monkey. When a horoscope chart contains a Triple

Harmony, it is regarded as being exceptionally favourable. The three Animal Signs work together to give insights into a person's latent potential and prospects.

If we imagine the 12 Animal Signs being arranged round a clockface at the hour positions, the three Animal Signs that combine to make one of the Triple Harmonies stand four hours apart. In the example of the Rat, Dragon and Monkey, if the Rat is placed at the 12 o'clock position, the Dragon and Monkey will be at the four o'clock and eight o'clock

The North Triangle: Water

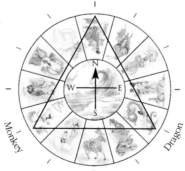

The West Triangle: Metal

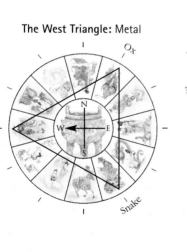

The East Triangle: Wood

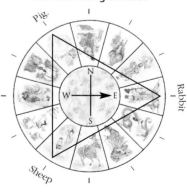

The South Triangle: Fire

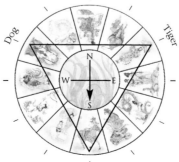

positions respectively, completing an equilateral triangle. The Triangles consist of Rat – Dragon – Monkey; Ox – Snake – Rooster; Tiger – Horse – Dog; Rabbit – Sheep – Pig.

As each of the Four Triangles points to a different one of the four cardinal points, north, east, south or west, each of the Triple Harmonies can be called by the compass direction to which the triangle points. So the Rat, Dragon and Monkey group can be called the North Triangle, since the Rat stands at the north position.

ANIMALS, SEASONS AND ELEMENTS

ANIMAL	SEASON	DIRECTION	DEGREES	ELEMENT
Rat	Winter	North	350°–10°	Water
Ox	Earth		20°–40°	Earth
Tiger	Approach of Spring		50°–70°	Wood
Rabbit	Spring	East	80°–100°	Wood
Dragon	Earth		110°–130°	Earth
Snake	Approach of Summer		140°–160°	Fire
Horse	Summer	South	170°–190°	Fire
Sheep	Earth		200°–220°	Earth
Monkey	Approach of Autumn		230°–250°	Metal
Rooster	Autumn	West	260°–280°	Metal
Dog	Earth		290°–310°	Earth
Pig	Approach of Winter		320°–340°	Water

THE SEASONAL ELEMENTS

Chinese astrologers usually refer to the Elements associated with the directions rather than the directions themselves. In Chinese philosophy there are Five Elements, each associated with the times of day, the seasons, and compass directions. We have already met the Earth Element, in the section about the months and the seasons. The other four Elements are Water, which is cold and wet and associated with winter and the north; its opposite, Fire, which is appropriate for south and the summer season; Wood, representing east and the budding and growth of plants in the spring; and Metal, representing west, reminding us of the scythes and sickles used at harvest time. The Earth Element is a case on its own; as we saw, the Earth season appears at the end of the familiar yearly seasons.

The table above shows the 12 Animal Signs, with their respective seasons, directions and Elements. The directions do not match the Western compass exactly, so approximate tolerances are given in compass degrees.

When we consider each of the three individual animals that make one of the Four Triangles we discover something remarkable: the names of the animals were not adopted randomly, but chosen because they had a deeper symbolic and astrological significance, not only individually, but when linked together. There are three signs that are all associated with inventiveness and resourcefulness, three that relate to family home and children, three hunters and three merchants.

Here are a few brief remarks about the qualities of these four very important combinations of three Animal Signs.

THE NORTH TRIANGLE
RAT – DRAGON – MONKEY

Taken on its own, the Rat qualities are intuition, innovation and creativity. But without any practical support or stimulus, the Rat's creative ideas tend to exist merely as a few remarks jotted on paper, or at worst, remain unformulated. The Dragon has an effusive and spectacular personality and lifestyle, but needs material to work with; a wonderful actor, maybe, with plenty of flair, but nonetheless the Dragon always needs a script. The Monkey has plenty of technical ability and an enquiring, indeed inquisitive mind, coupled with a manual dexterity that the other two members of the Water Triangle may lack. Yet it often feels frustrated by a restrictive environment, with the result that its undoubted skills are wasted aimlessly or put to the wrong use.

If you put the Rat, the Dragon and the Monkey together you have all the ingredients for a creative genius who has a well-developed talent for finding opportunities and exploiting them, and the ability to make things work. Thus, from this North Triangle springs the raw material for a successful inventor, or manufacturer, or an innovative designer. Yet there is more than this to consider. The north, signifying winter, influences the areas of media, communication and correspondence. So when these three factors which make the Water Triangle are together in a person's horoscope, they stimulate a restless undercurrent that urges travel, change and spontaneous action.

THE EAST TRIANGLE
RABBIT – SHEEP – PIG

These three animals all have a Yin or feminine quality. The Rabbit shows a caring personality, caring for children, animals or the under-privileged. The Sheep is the animal that looks after female interests, in particular, partnerships and marriage. The Pig is concerned with the comforts of the home and its interior furnishings. Assembled together, they form a group with strong home and family ties, suggesting happy partnerships, a welcoming hearth, a table laden with good food, many children and grandchildren.

The east is represented by the Wood Element, which itself is a sign of growth, nutrition and good health. It shows peace, gentleness and tranquillity. These three signs in a horoscope reveal someone who yearns to settle down and raise a family.

The East Triangle person may be drawn to nursing, medicine or child welfare as a career. Those without families may seek to find other ways that they can substitute for not having children of their own, perhaps through teaching or looking after animals.

THE SOUTH TRIANGLE
TIGER – HORSE – DOG

The South Triangle joins together three animals that are all connected with hunting. The south represents summer, the Element Fire and masculine attributes: the very opposite of the gentle, feminine East Triangle. The three animals combine to create an ambitious and competitive individual, determined to succeed at whatever cost. The Element Fire is also associated with intelligence, so while the obvious result of the influence of the South Triangle may be a ruthless streak, or someone dedicated to competitive sports, the strong Fire influence may be directed in another positive way, producing a brilliant mind.

The South Triangle person will pursue any career in which there is the stimulus of rivalry and the need to succeed, and may be drawn to the contentious world of politics.

THE WEST TRIANGLE
OX – SNAKE – ROOSTER

This trio may seem unlikely company, but together they form a startlingly effective business team. The west is associated with the autumn and the Element Metal, which itself suggests the clink of coins rattling into the till. In this group, it is the flamboyant Rooster that is the public face of the business venture, in charge of promotion and the product image. But no matter how successful the advertising, or how great the demand, there has to be something to sell. The hard-working and dedicated Ox turns to the production side, and so keeps the partnership on a sound practical footing. Meanwhile, the account books and legal matters will be managed efficiently by the analytical Snake.

A business partnership comprised of these three people will make a very successful team, while those individuals who have these three signs in their horoscope charts will prove to be very shrewd and astute when handling the financial side of their professional lives.

PRACTICAL APPLICATION OF THE TRIANGLES

In the previous chapter, when the mutual effect of pairs of Animal Signs was considered, we could see that the two Animal Signs might represent (a) two time factors in the same horoscope, or (b) a particular period of time and a person or even (c) two different people. We can add another possibility to these three, that of the compass direction.

The beneficial effects of the triangles may come together in one horoscope, but they might also come into force when two of the Animal Signs are found in a horoscope, and the third Animal Sign is suggested in the horoscope of another person, or a period of time, or even a direction.

For example, a person who had an Ox and a Snake in their horoscope might improve the chances of business success if a Rooster was present. This could happen if that person was joined by a business partner born in the year of the Rooster, or the business was expanded in 2005 (a Rooster year) or if they moved to a premises in a westerly direction, west being the compass point associated with the Rooster.

THE THREE CROSSES

Earlier, we saw that when two Animal Signs were opposite to each other on the clockface, this made an unfavourable combination. Either the seasons clash (winter against summer, spring against autumn) or the Earths clash (Ox and Sheep, Dog and Dragon). Also unfavourable, but not as unfortunate, are the cases when two Animal Signs stand three hours apart, or at right angles to each other, as is the case with the Rat and Rabbit, or the Rat

and Rooster. The table on this page shows the hostile and adverse combinations for each of the animals.

What is remarkable, however, is that when all four hostile or adverse Animal Signs are together in the same horoscope, instead of it being an omen of doom, the negative influences neutralize each other, producing a harmonious accord.

There are three such harmonious crosses: the Four Compass Directions, the Four Approaches to the Seasons, and the Four Earths. Chinese astrologers have given these poetic names, which are found below.

UNFAVOURABLE ALLIANCES

ANIMAL	HOSTILE	ADVERSE	ADVERSE
RAT	Horse	Rabbit	Rooster
OX	Sheep	Dragon	Dog
TIGER	Monkey	Snake	Pig
RABBIT	Rooster	Horse	Rat
DRAGON	Dog	Sheep	Ox
SNAKE	Pig	Monkey	Tiger
HORSE	Rat	Rooster	Rabbit
SHEEP	Ox	Dog	Dragon
MONKEY	Tiger	Pig	Snake
ROOSTER	Rabbit	Rat	Horse
DOG	Dragon	Ox	Sheep
PIG	Snake	Tiger	Monkey

THE FOUR COMPASS DIRECTIONS, OR FLOWERS OF LOVE

When the four Animal Signs in the horoscope chart are the Rat, Rabbit, Horse and Rooster, marking the compass points, it symbolizes the Emperor at the Centre, ruling over the four directions. Together, they denote power and fame, and someone whose name is destined to be remembered. Collectively they are also known by the rather misleading name of the Four Flowers of Love, the implication being that someone who has riches and power will never be short of love. The 'flowers of love' signify a person's numerous children or grandchildren.

THE FOUR APPROACHES TO THE SEASONS, OR COACHING POSTS

The Tiger, Snake, Monkey and Pig represent the four Approaches to the Seasons, even though only one of the Animal Signs will actually belong to the month. The poetic name for the four signs is the Four Coaching Posts, that is, the halting places on a journey. Long ago it would have meant a change of horses, or an overnight stop at an inn; in today's world it could imply a change of planes at an airport. These four signs together in a horoscope signify an obligation to travel long distances, and often.

THE FOUR EARTHS, OR LITERARY MERIT

The cross known as the Literary Merit comprises the four 'Earth' Animals: Ox, Dragon, Sheep and Dog. Appearing in a horoscope, it is a sign of creative talent revealed by artistic and literary gifts, such as the writing of serious fiction or poetry, by musical ability, especially in composition and interpretation, or by expressive painting. The Earth Element, representing contemplation, reveals that the created works have a meditative quality.

The Four Compass Directions

The Four Approaches to the Seasons
The Four Coaching Posts

The Four Earths
Literary Merit

DEFAULTING SIGNS

The Three Crosses are special cases, and their appearance in a horoscope is not a common occurrence. It is, however, quite usual to find three of the components of a cross in the horoscope, with the fourth Animal Sign either at another position in the horoscope (an example being Rat, Rabbit, Rooster and Sheep) or doubling one of the other three Animal Signs already present in the cross (such as Rat, Rabbit and two Rooster signs).

In both of the examples given above, the fourth Animal Sign, the Horse, is missing from the cross, and in this situation it can be said to be defaulting.

Defaulting signs are just as significant by their absence as they would be if they were present. First think of the qualities normally associated with the missing sign, then consider what would be the effect on the character if these qualities were lacking.

When an Animal Sign is in default, it can be introduced externally to redress the imbalance. One way in which this happens is when it is prominent in a partner's horoscope. Another way is by moving house in the direction of the Animal Sign. Thus, if the missing animal were the Horse, representing the south, a relocation southwards would restore the missing Horse factor.

Here are a few remarks on the significance of each of the Animal Signs when in default.

THE FOUR COMPASS DIRECTIONS, OR FLOWERS OF LOVE

Rat, Rabbit, Horse and Rooster

Rat in default. The absence of the late-night Rat, with its ability to chew over figures, shows that the subject of the horoscope needs to take time to reckon the consequences of any actions. There may be a reluctance to move forward or take the initiative, but the most frequently observed symptom of Rat-withdrawal is a dislike of figures.

Rabbit in default. The missing Rabbit, associated with children and health, would suggest that these areas could be the source of problems. The management and control of junior members of the family may prove troublesome; it also suggests that the subject may suffer from unhealthy internal organs.

Horse in default. The Horse suggests physical strength, its absence a weakness in the limbs. As the Horse is also associated with social and sporting activities, the person may suffer undue shyness or be awkward with strangers.

Rooster in default. The Rooster marks the end of the day, a time to cease everyday toil and enjoy pleasant pastimes. With this factor missing, the horoscope suggests a restless individual who finds it difficult to settle, and may suffer needless worries and anxieties.

THE FOUR APPROACHES TO THE SEASONS, OR COACHING POSTS

Tiger, Snake, Monkey and Pig

Tiger in default. It may be a wonderful idea to travel the world, but this dream will not be achieved if the subject constantly gives in to outside pressure. Older relations may make demands on the subject's time and loyalty, or the subject may feel restrained by work or family commitments.

Snake in default. Travelling to exotic locations requires more than time and money; there are often diplomatic and political obstacles. Although these are not as restrictive as in former times, there could still be legal obstacles preventing freedom of travel.

Monkey in default. The Monkey, master of manual and verbal skills, is not on hand to help. It would be unwise to contemplate settling in a foreign country without being familiar with the language, or if planning to settle abroad, it would be vital to be adept in such crafts as carpentry, plumbing and building.

Pig in default. The Pig, symbol of home comforts, is not at home. The remaining three Coaching Posts suggest that the journey through life is not focused. The horoscope reveals a nomadic existence. Finding the right partner or location could remedy the sense of being cast adrift.

THE FOUR EARTHS, OR LITERARY MERIT

Ox, Dragon, Sheep and Dog

Ox in default. As the Ox signifies stamina and perseverance, with this aspect of the cross missing, the gifted artistic genius lacks the will or determination to see a work carried through to its conclusion. Many brilliant projects will be undertaken, but left incomplete.

Dragon in default. The Dragon is a sign of extrovert daring; it is needed to complete the Literary Merit group, otherwise the confidence to strike out in an altogether new direction is lacking, and this prevents untapped talents from developing.

Sheep in default. The missing factor here is the one that governs home and marriage. The absence of the Sheep indicates a reluctance to settle down in a family, or difficulties in forming close relationships. But when the right partner is found, that is one in whose horoscope the Sheep is prominent, family harmony is assured.

Dog in default. Difficulties in setting up a home may be thought to be due to the pressure of family commitments, but the real reason is a dissatisfaction with the location and environment. The obvious solution to the problem is to move away from the present situation to a location that would bring the missing Dog into the horoscope.

THE SIX MANSIONS

In the chapter introducing the 12 Animal Signs, occasional references were made to the fact that the Animal Signs were in pairs, Yang and Yin. From the traditional qualities accorded to the 12 Animal Signs of the Chinese horoscope, it can be inferred that they fall into six clear divisions. To avoid confusion with the 12 'houses' of Western astrology, or the 12 'fate palaces' in later Chinese astrology (which in any case are a borrowing from Western astrology), these six qualities – Creativity, Expansion, Magic, Gender, Skill and Home – are here called the Six Mansions.

The table on the left provides a reminder of the basic qualities of each of the 12 Animal Signs, their polarity (whether Yang or Yin), and the Mansion to which they belong.

When two Animal Signs belonging to the same Mansion are in a horoscope chart, they are able to work together to produce completion. If Rat and Ox are together, this shows someone with ideas who is able to follow these ideas through to their conclusion. A blend of Tiger and Rabbit produces a person who knows when it is best to be sternly disciplinarian, and when it is better to use tactful diplomacy. When Dragon and Snake meet, this is a balance of the outrageously extrovert and the modestly retiring, someone who knows when it is time to put on a show, and when to fade silently into the background. The Horse and Sheep are both concerned with gender issues; the Horse wanting an active and vigorous social life, while the Sheep values family commitments. With Monkey and Rooster in the horoscope, technical design and practicality is matched with good presentation. Finally, with regard to the home, the Dog is concerned with the exterior of the building, and the Pig with its interior furnishings.

COMPLEMENTARY SIGNS

ANIMAL	POLARITY	MANSION
Rat	Yang	inventiveness
		CREATIVITY
Ox	Yin	determination
Tiger	Yang	authority
		EXPANSION
Rabbit	Yin	diplomacy
Dragon	Yang	excitement
		MAGIC
Snake	Yin	discretion
Horse	Yang	comradeship
		GENDER
Sheep	Yin	partnership
Monkey	Yang	craftmanship
		SKILL
Rooster	Yin	artistry
Dog	Yang	exterior
		HOME
Pig	Yin	interior

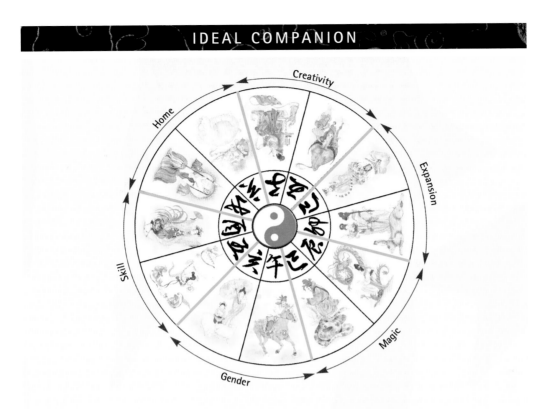

THE SIX MANSIONS

THE HAIRPINS

We saw that it is unfavourable when two Animal Signs are on opposite sides of the horoscope chart, representing opposing seasons. It reveals stresses between the two signs that are in opposition. But if one of the opposing signs is combined with the other Animal Signs in the same Mansion, then the two adjacent Animal Signs attack the third. Thus, if a particular set of circumstances. brought the Rat, Ox and Sheep together, the Rat and Ox, as a pair in the same Mansion, would overcome the solitary Sheep. As the Sheep represents partnership or marriage, such a combination of signs could indicate a future

divorce. Or, if instead of the Sheep the opposed sign were a Horse, it would signify disloyal companions or the loss of friends.

In a horoscope chart, the combination of two adjacent signs and an opposite one resembles a hairpin (see page 122).

Note that the effect of the hairpins only occurs when the two adjacent signs belong to the same Mansion. In the case of the Ox and Tiger, although these are adjacent Animal Signs, they are from different Mansions and belong to different seasons, so they are unable to join forces against the poor Sheep. The effect of the 'hairpins' is summed up on pages 122–3.

RAT AND OX OPPOSING SHEEP

As the Sheep represents marriage and family partnerships, this aspect of the horoscope is weakened. If all three signs are in the same person's horoscope, it indicates a reluctance to enter into a permanent commitment; if either the Rat or the Ox belongs to the partnership, the relationship will be an uncomfortable one.

RAT AND OX OPPOSING HORSE

The convivial Horse will be upset to lose friends, through an action, rightly, wrongly or mistakenly perceived as unacceptable or disloyal. If the Ox and Horse are in the same horoscope, but the Rat is an outside influence (another person, or perhaps a Rat year) the effect will be more marked because of its suddenness. If the Ox is part of the person's horoscope, it shows that lifelong friendships are unlikely, perhaps through frequent changes of location for professional reasons.

TIGER AND RABBIT OPPOSING MONKEY

Since the Monkey represents manual skills, if these three signs are present in a horoscope, it shows problems with the use of the hands in later life. If the Rabbit and Monkey are present, there are dangers of injury to the limbs in Tiger or Rabbit years.

TIGER AND RABBIT OPPOSING ROOSTER

The confidence of the Rooster is lessened when opposed by Tiger and Rabbit. An inner confusion leads to problems in expressing ideas

RAT, OX AND SHEEP HAIRPIN

concisely, with a tendency to talk too fast rather than clearly and carefully.

DRAGON AND SNAKE OPPOSING DOG

Finding a suitable home is never an easy task; it is even more difficult when the configuration of Dog, Dragon and Snake come together. In one horoscope, it shows restlessness and unease in any permanent location. For someone contemplating a house purchase, a date which has the combination of Dog, Dragon and Snake is highly inadvisable, as it suggests legal problems will ensue.

DRAGON AND SNAKE OPPOSING PIG

The supernatural qualities of the Dragon and Snake opposed to the Pig affect the enjoyment of home life. In some cases, there may be an uncomfortable feeling that the home is haunted, or beset by ill-luck. If the Dog is present in the horoscope, or present in the horoscope of the partner, this will counteract the adverse atmosphere. Sometimes a more positive effect of this is the choice of an exotic career involving a complete break from roots.

HORSE AND SHEEP OPPOSING RAT

The Rat's clear-thinking and initiative are dulled when opposed by the Horse-Sheep combination. There are likely to be problems in forming relationships, both personal and social, with persons of either sex, and a failure to communicate properly affects the Rat's ability to concentrate.

HORSE AND SHEEP OPPOSING OX

A period marked by the Sheep and Horse signs is a dangerous time for the Ox, as the latter's usually reliable determination decays into indecisiveness and irresolution. If all three signs are in the same horoscope, the Ox will often continue along a routine path almost as a compulsion, rather than with any clear objective in mind.

MONKEY AND ROOSTER OPPOSING TIGER

If all three signs are present in one horoscope, it shows authority being undermined. Enemies will quickly perceive any weakness in character, leading to exploitation. It is necessary to cultivate firmness and resolution. People born in Tiger years need to be particularly watchful at times when periods ruled by the Monkey and Rooster coincide.

MONKEY AND ROOSTER OPPOSING RABBIT

The Rabbit, associated with childhood, is adversely affected by the Monkey and Rooster pair. It suggests a troubled or unhappy childhood, or in later life difficulties in understanding children who may be perceived as an unwelcome nuisance. In contrast, yet another consequence of the conflict may be problems in raising children or possibly in conceiving in the first instance. Introducing the Tiger factor to this combination would neutralize the destructive effects of the Monkey-Rooster influence.

DOG AND PIG OPPOSING DRAGON

The Dragon may have wonderful ideas for the future, but these are held in contempt by members of the family who regard such far-fetched notions with disdain. There may be such a strong attachment to home life that plans that could bring fame and financial rewards are abandoned in favour of something more conventional and urbane. It is sad when enthusiasm gives way to apathy.

DOG AND PIG OPPOSING SNAKE

The Snake combines meticulous attention to detail with discretion bordering on secrecy. These traits, highly desirable qualities for the scholar and researcher, are eroded by the Dog and Pig in opposition. The scrupulous precision that one expects fades, and the result is carelessness and negligence. There is a desire to spend more money on home decoration and furnishings than can reasonably be afforded.

THE LIFE CYCLE

A LIFE VIEW

Many people find that the most fascinating aspect of Chinese astrology is its ability to provide a complete overview of someone's life. We have seen how the basic factors of the horoscope tell us whether certain years, months, days or even times are likely to be favourable or otherwise. Now we shall look at the Life Cycle, which helps the horoscope interpreter to make forecasts for the subject's whole life in a series of ten-year periods. Some Chinese astrologers refer to these ten-year periods as the 'Luck Pillars' or 'Fortune Columns'.

Astrologers spoke of the Life Cycle columns more than a thousand years ago. The method is usually called the Ziping method, after a celebrated 10th-century soothsayer, Xu Ziping, who wrote a book commenting on the 'three kinds of Fate'. Unfortunately, we know hardly anything at all about Xu Ziping's life, but the technique he described to calculate the Fortune Columns has remained unchanged in the centuries since his lifetime. The horoscopes described in the Chinese novel *Jin Ping Mei* follow exactly the same methods as those described here.

THE TEN-YEAR FORTUNE COLUMNS

Just as a year is divided into months, so a person's life is divided into ten-yearly periods. The Fortune Columns are the months of that life. Those who are born in a spring month begin their lives in the spring period of their existence; they are like cherry blossom, which brings joy in its early years, grows unremarked in the summer, and then presents luscious fruit in the autumn. Similarly, those who are born in winter are like bamboo, which withstands the blasts of winter and the heat of summer; so the lessons learnt in the winter of their lives help them to deal with whatever difficult situations face them in the spring, summer and autumn years that follow.

For this reason, the ten-year period during which a person is born (the Natal Column) has the same Animal Sign as the month of birth. Thus, if someone were born on 10 March, which falls in the Rabbit month (see page 48), then the sign for that person's Natal Column would also be the Rabbit.

FORWARD OR BACKWARD SEQUENCE

The Animal Sign for the next Fortune Column depends on whether the motion of the sequence is forward (in which case the next column would be the Dragon), or backward (in which case the next column would be the Tiger). Discovering if the sequence goes backward or forward is a simple matter of considering two things: whether the person is male or female, and whether the year of birth is Yang or Yin.

*As the seasons of spring, summer and autumn
follow in an unchanging order, so the cycles of life
follow in a predictable sequence.*

As a reminder, these Animals are Yang:
Rat, Tiger, Dragon, Horse, Monkey and Dog; and
these are Yin: Ox, Rabbit, Snake, Sheep, Rooster
and Pig.

Now here's the tricky bit. If the Yang or
Yin quality of the person and the year are both
the same, then the sequence goes forward. But
if the Yang and Yin are different, the sequence
goes backward. As an example, for a man
(Yang) born in 1972 (a Rat year, therefore
Yang), or for a woman (Yin) born in 1973 (Ox,
Yin) the sequence goes forward. But for a man
(Yang) born in 1973 (Yin) or a woman (Yin)
born in 1972 (Yang), the sequence goes
backward, because Yin and Yang are mixed.

You need to remember whether the
sequence goes forward or backward, as this
information will be used again shortly.

THE STARTING AGE

A person's birth happens during the ten-year
period of the Natal Fortune Column. Therefore
the following ten-year periods must begin their
course at some point during the first ten years
of life. The age at which these periods
commence depends on the date of the month
the person was born, and whether the 'motion'
of the sequence is forward or backward.

A Chinese solar month has about 30 days,
which can be reckoned as ten periods of three
days. As each ten-year Fortune Column

represents a 'month' of life, it follows that each
year of the ten-year period is represented by
three days of a calendar month.

It follows that just as the month in which
a person is born symbolizes the start of the
ten-year periods, the three-day period in which
the birthday occurs represents the age when
the next ten-year period begins.

To find this starting age, count the
number of days between the birthday and the
start of the astrological month and divide
by three (since one year of life is represented
by three days). Whether we count forward
to the next month, or backward to the previous
month depends on the type of motion. If the
motion is forward, count forward the number
of days to the start of the next monthly
Animal Sign; if the motion is backward, count
backward to the start of the current Animal
Sign. Dividing the total number of days
between the birthday and the start of the
monthly Animal Sign by three (rounding up or
down to the nearest whole number) gives the
age at which the next Fortune Column begins.

March					1	2	3
	4	5	6	7	8	9	10
	11	12	13	14	15	16	17
	18	19	20	21	22	23	24
	25	26	27	28	29	30	31
April	1	2	3	4	5	6	7
	8	9	10	11	12	13	14

Suppose a man's birthday was 10 March 1972. The man and 1972 (a Rat year) are both Yang, so the motion is forward. The Animal Sign for the month of birth is the Rabbit, and the Rabbit month begins on 6 March (see the table on page 48).

Since the motion is forward, we count forward the number of days to the next (Dragon) month, which begins on 5 April, 26 days altogether. Dividing 26 by three gives nine (the figure can be rounded up or down to the nearest whole number), which means that the starting age for his next Fortune Column is nine, and because the motion is forward, the Animal Sign for the next ten-year period or Fortune Column will be the Dragon, which is the next sign after the Rabbit.

But for a woman (Yin) born on the same day, the motion would be backward, since the Rat year is Yang. This would mean that to find the woman's starting age, we would count backward from 10 March to the start of the Rabbit month on 6 March.

This amounts to four days, which divided by three gives one (rounding down to the nearest whole number). Thus, the woman's starting age is one and, as the motion is backward, the Animal Sign for her next Fortune Column is the Tiger, the sign before the Rabbit.

The Ten-Year Fortune Columns follow in sequence at ten-yearly intervals. Each period belongs to the Animal Sign that follows in sequence, either forward or backward, as above. Therefore, for the man whose birthday was 10 March 1972, and whose Animal Sign for the month of birth was the Rabbit, the Fortune Columns would be set as follows:

AGE	(NATAL MONTH)	9	19	29	39	49	59	69	79	89
ANIMAL	RABBIT	Dragon	Snake	Horse	Sheep	Monkey	Rooster	Dog	Pig	Rat

For the woman with the same birthdate, because she is female (Yin) in a Rat (Yang) year, the Fortune Columns start at age one, and the Animal Signs run in reverse order:

AGE	(NATAL MONTH)	1	11	21	31	41	51	61	71	81
ANIMAL	RABBIT	Tiger	Ox	Rat	Pig	Dog	Rooster	Monkey	Sheep	Horse

INTERPRETING
THE LIFE CYCLE

The horoscope chart can be perceived as a picture showing how the four factors of time, day, month and year focus on the moment a person is born. The Life Cycle, however, is like a continuous scroll. Because it is linear it is interpreted in a way that uses a slightly different perspective.

When interpreting the Life Cycle, the key factor is the day of birth. This is a much more personal factor than the year in which someone is born.

But the calculation for the Animal Sign of the day of birth tells us more than just the Animal Sign; it also tells us something else about this key factor: the Stem, or Element of the day. Both the Animal Sign and its Element can be used to evaluate the favourable qualities of the Fortune Column.

USING THE ANIMAL
SIGN OF THE DAY

Begin by comparing the Animal Sign for the day with the Animal Signs for each of the Fortune Columns. This gives the first outlook on whether a particular ten-year period is generally favourable or otherwise. For example, if the daily Animal Sign were a Sheep, then those Fortune Columns that harmonized with the Sheep, such as those that belonged to the Pig or Rabbit, would be generally favourable periods, while a ten-year period ruled by the unsympathetic Dog, the bizarre Dragon or the stolid Ox (which opposes the Sheep) would indicate a less favourable ten-year period.

Within any particular ten-year period, the individual years can be reviewed as shown in Chapters 1 and 2. Most people tend to be more interested in the present ten-year period of their lives, firstly to see if their horoscope bears out the events of their recent past, and secondly to find out what the immediate future holds for them.

USING THE STEM OR
ELEMENT OF THE DAY

The Stem or Element of the day is the essence of the Life Cycle interpretation. It represents the personal self; sometimes there are favourable periods in life, at other times it is important to tread carefully. At times the self may be supportive of others, at other times it may need support and encouragement.

Therefore the Stem or Element of the day is compared with the Animal Sign for the Fortune Column period to find a more specific interpretation of the prospects for that ten-year period.

The Stem or Element of the Day is revealed by the last digit of the daily animal cycle number, given in Table C (Animal Signs for the 60-Day Cycle) on page 61.

Examine the Table of Stems on page 130, and cross-refer the Stem and Element of the day to each of the Animal Signs for the ten-yearly Fortune Columns. This will yield a code letter that refers to one of the paragraphs that follow on page 131. Read the relevant paragraph to establish whether that phase in the Life Cycle will be generally favourable or destructive for the subject.

FORTUNE COLUMN CODE LETTER A

The Personal Element receives benefit from that of the Fortune Column

Known to Chinese astrologers as the 'true seal', this is regarded as a highly advantageous period, bringing welcome outside support for favoured schemes. If you have had to wait for financial backing or official permission before plans could be carried out, this will soon be forthcoming.

FORTUNE COLUMN CODE LETTER B

The Personal Element exhausts that of the Fortune Column

This is a period when it is necessary to draw on your savings or use outside resources. Take care not to exhaust these, as the well is not bottomless. In dealing with other people, it would be wise to take account of their feelings and vulnerability.

FORTUNE COLUMN CODE LETTER C

The Personal Element is the same as that of the Fortune Column

It is best to use your initiative and to trust your instincts during this very favourable period. In your career, there is a strong positive move forward. It is a constructive phase, and everything should be done to harness the very positive resources available.

TABLE OF STEMS

FORTUNE COLUMN	DAY–STEM	1 YANG Wood	2 YIN Wood	3 YANG Fire	4 YIN Fire	5 YANG Earth	6 YIN Earth	7 YANG Metal	8 YIN Metal	9 YANG Water	10 YIN Water
Rat	Water	A	K	H	J	E	B	F	G	C	D
Ox	Earth	B	E	G	F	D	C	A	K	J	H
Tiger	Wood	C	D	A	K	H	J	E	B	F	G
Rabbit	Wood	D	C	K	A	J	H	B	E	G	F
Dragon	Earth	E	B	G	F	C	D	K	A	H	J
Snake	Fire	F	G	C	D	K	A	H	J	E	B
Horse	Fire	G	F	D	C	A	K	J	H	B	E
Sheep	Earth	B	E	G	F	D	C	A	K	J	H
Monkey	Metal	H	J	E	B	F	G	C	D	A	K
Rooster	Metal	J	H	B	E	G	F	D	C	K	A
Dog	Earth	E	B	G	F	C	D	K	A	H	J
Pig	Water	K	A	J	H	B	E	G	F	D	C

FORTUNE COLUMN CODE LETTER D

The Personal Element is the same as that of the Fortune Column

This is a very favourable period both for family life and career prospects. Personal happiness may come from joyous relationships, or the achievement of a long-standing ambition.

FORTUNE COLUMN CODE LETTER E

The Personal Element exhausts that of the Fortune Column

During this financially difficult period, avoid risky investments, and dangerous sporting activities. Do not take holidays in places that are politically unsafe, or where the environment is unhealthy.

FORTUNE COLUMN CODE LETTER F

The Personal Element donates to that of the Fortune Column

This is a period when more goes out than comes in. Avoid extravagance. It is best to deal in certainties rather than take risks. Superficial ailments should not be ignored. When in doubt, ask for advice.

FORTUNE COLUMN CODE LETTER G

The Personal Element donates to that of the Fortune Column

Although this may be a time of heavy expenditure, there are sound reasons for this. Marriage, children, education and house-purchase are all examples of sensible investment for the future. There should be no anxiety. This is a favourable period as far as personal relationships are concerned, but it would be wise to avoid letting your partner become extravagant.

FORTUNE COLUMN CODE LETTER H

The Personal Element is overpowered by that of the Fortune Column

Much depends on your attitude and moral stance; there is much to be gained at the expense of other people's losses. There are chances to make great profit, and to take the offer of advancement to higher position, but this will cause resentment and jealousy among rivals.

FORTUNE COLUMN CODE LETTER J

The Personal Element is overpowered by that of the Fortune Column

What may appear to be a calamity at first will turn out to be a benefit in the end. Patience is required, and a firm determination is needed to survive the stormy passage. Eventually, the wisdom of remaining steadfast will be apparent, and any changes that are imposed will lead to unexpected success.

FORTUNE COLUMN CODE LETTER K

The Personal Element receives benefit from that of the Fortune Column

During this period there are unexpected benefits from an unlikely source; the indications are usually financial gains through legacies or gains through a lottery, but sometimes the rewards come in less conventional forms.

APPENDIX I
CASTING AND INTERPRETING
HOROSCOPE

To get the feel of the way a Chinese horoscope is set up, first choose a few birthdates of people born after 21 February in any year, and whose birthdays fall on the tenth of the month or later.

Of course, it's bound to be the case that the very people whose horoscopes you want to do have their birthdays in January, or else they were born on the second of the month. Be patient. We'll tackle those later. For the moment, choose birthdates which fall within the defined limits while you get to grips with the essential process of setting up a Chinese horoscope, and finding out what it means.

Assemble all your facts, put them into a table, then construct a chart similar to the one shown below and make a note of the Animal Signs on it.

Name	
Date of birth	Time of birth
❶ Animal Sign for the YEAR	Y
❷ Animal Sign for the MONTH	M
❸ *Number of the day (1–60)* Animal Sign for the DAY	D
❹ Animal Sign for the HOUR	H

STEP 1
Use the table on page 22 to find the Animal Sign for the YEAR. Make a note of it on line 1 of your chart.

STEP 2
Use the table on page 48 to find the Animal Sign for the MONTH. Make a note of it on line 2 of your chart. Some hints regarding the significance of the Animal Sign for the month are given on the page listed in the table.

STEP 3
Use the table on page 60 to find the Animal Sign for the DAY. Make a note of it on line 3 of your chart.

STEP 4
Use the table on page 76 to find the Animal Sign for the HOUR. Make a note of it on line 4 of your chart.

THE CHART OF THE FOUR ANIMALS

You now have the Animal Signs for the year, month, day and hour, the foundation of the Chinese horoscope. Even at this early stage you can use it to make an assessment of the person's character, strengths and weaknesses.

Make a copy of the diagram below, and on it mark the positions of the four Animal Signs you have found with the letters H, D, M, Y. To see if there are any harmonies or contrasts, join these with lines. If the lines make any recognizable patterns, such as the Triangles or Crosses, make a note of these as well. You are now ready to assess the person's situation. Decide which Animal Signs are going to be helpful and which are likely to foreshadow problems for the person.

From the Animal Sign for the year you can make a general character assessment and determine the best kind of life partner for the person. From the sign for the month you can judge the relationship with parents and superiors, and from the sign for the hour, the relationship with children and subordinates. Now you can use the Animal Sign for the day to construct the Life Cycle. The pattern of signs should give a clue about career potential, revealing skills and weaknesses.

From your knowledge of the favourable and unfavourable signs, you will be able to assess which ten-year periods are most likely to be successful, as well as those periods when the person should take care not to get involved in risky ventures.

As you become more practised you will be able to unravel more and more of people's life-enhancing potentials, offering advice and encouragement over the whole spectrum of daily quandaries.

EXAMPLE OF HOW TO
SET UP A HOROSCOPE

lvis Aaron Presley was born on 8 January 1935, in Tupelo, Mississippi. The time was 'shortly before dawn', which would have been about 5.20 am. If an incense stick had been lit at the moment of his birth, and extinguished at his first cry, a Chinese soothsayer would have declared that he was born during the Rabbit hour, which lasts from 5.00 am to 7.00 am.

This brief review provides a step-by-step guide to the construction of a Chinese horoscope Life Cycle chart, with suggestions on the ways that the charts can be interpreted.

THE YEAR ANIMAL

❶ First turn to page 138, the Table of Chinese Solar and Lunar Signs, to find the Animal Sign for 1935. As 8 January occurs before the Chinese New Year we look in the first column to find the Animal Sign for the year, which is the DOG.

THE MONTH ANIMAL

❶ Consult the table on page 48 in the section on the Animal Sign for the month.

❷ The start of the Ox month is 6 January, so there is no need to check the supplementary table (Dates of the Solar Months) on pages 140–1.

❸ Thus the month animal is the OX.

THE DAY ANIMAL

❶ Follow the method on pages 60–1 to find the Animal Sign for the day, and also the special stem characteristics revealed by the cyclical number.

❷ From Table A, the code number for 1935 is 13

❸ From Table B, the code number for January is 0

❹ For the eighth day add 8

Total: 13 + 0 + 8 = 21

❺ From Table C the daily Animal Sign for 21 is the MONKEY

❻ The Cyclical Sign is 21, Stem 1, Yang–Wood Monkey

THE HOUR ANIMAL

❶ From the chart on page 76 we see the Animal Sign for the hour to be the RABBIT.

THE HOROSCOPE CHART

We now have the basic information required for setting up the horoscope chart and interpreting it.

The obvious way to begin interpreting the horoscope is to look first at the Animal Sign for the year, and make a general assessment of character for those born in the year of the Dog. 'In choosing a career, military service and security roles are alluded to.' One of the most outstanding episodes in Elvis Presley's life was his refusal to avoid his military service obligations. Another pertinent fact is that his first singing success, which brought him a second prize in a talent contest at the age of ten, was his rendering of a song about a dog,

'Old Shep', which was to remain a popular favourite throughout his career.

The other Animal Signs, for the time, day and month, are added to the chart. A note is made of any obvious harmonies or clashes, and in particular, any patterns, such as triangles or crosses that could indicate something special.

In Elvis Presley's horoscope there are no strong harmonies or triangles, nor for that matter are there any clashes with signs directly opposite each other. The Dog year has a favourable aspect with the Monkey day (both Yang signs); and on the opposite side of the chart the Ox month forms a favourable aspect with the Rabbit hour (both Yin signs). Although Yang and Yin are balanced, the Dog and the Ox are at odds with each other: '*Problems are inevitable but perseverance will eventually prove the most favourable course of action*.'

Yet there is something else about the horoscope that stands out immediately: it is remarkably symmetrical, and strongly reminiscent of the special Four Earths cross (see page 117), which is a sign of literary and artistic merit. Though he was not a Shakespeare, a Caravaggio or a Beethoven, Elvis Presley earned lasting fame through his enduring contribution to popular culture.

CHART ANALYSIS

Arranging the Animal Signs on the chart shows which ones are likely to be supportive and which ones indicate future problems. The Animal Sign for the year generally shows the trends for the greater part of a person's life, including career and marriage, while the Animal Sign for the hour is more concerned with shorter-term events. In Elvis Presley's chart, the supportive animals are: for the year (Dog), Tiger, Horse; for the month (Ox), Rooster, Snake; for the day (Monkey), Rat, Dragon; for the hour (Rabbit), Sheep, Pig.

The adverse signs, those opposite to the four Animal Signs in the horoscope, are Dragon, Sheep, Tiger and Rooster. Fortunately, as we have just seen, all four are also supportive, so their influence is a mixed one.

THE LIFE CYCLE CHART AND FORTUNE COLUMNS

Now we can look at the Fortune Columns in turn. From Elvis's day number we know his key Element and Animal to be Yang-Wood Monkey. In looking at the Fortune Columns, it is the Yang-Wood part of the day sign that is important. This Element has to be compared with the Elements of the Animal Signs in the Fortune Columns, rather than the actual Animal Signs themselves. But this is not a problem, as the combinations of Elements with the Animal Signs have already been prepared with the Table of Stems on page 130. Now, to calculate the Fortune Columns, see table below (left).

Elvis Presley was a man (Yang) born in a Dog year (Yang) so the motion is forward. He was born in an Ox month; the following Tiger month starts with 4 February.

By counting the number of days between 8 January and 4 February and dividing by three, we arrive at the starting age of nine.

The Life Cycle chart can be conveniently set out in this way: The key Element and Animal is the Yang-Wood Monkey.

Next we turn to the Table of Stems on page 130 to find the significance of each period.

Under the Stem 1 Yang-Wood column we have the code letters for the periods Ox to Snake, inclusive, see table below (right).

Throughout his childhood, Elvis Presley's family experienced hardship, revealed by the Life Cycle admonition B: 'a period when it is necessary to draw on one's savings.'

His first step into the musical world came when he was ten, in the Tiger period (code letter C) when 'it is best to use one's initiative ...a constructive phase...'

But Elvis still had to struggle to achieve his ambition: the Tiger is directly opposite the Monkey and some of the favourable influences of the period would be neutralized. From the age of 19 to 28 his career took off dramatically. Not only is the ten-year period generally favourable: '... *the achievement of a long-standing ambition...*' but it is ruled by the Rabbit, the same sign as that for his birth time.

During the next period (code letter E) the prospects are less favourable, and Elvis's popularity wanes considerably. Although the Dragon, which is favourable for the Monkey, is the Animal Sign ruling the period, and might normally be thought to be supportive, in the horoscope chart it is directly opposite to Elvis's year animal, the Dog.

Tragedy was to follow in the code letter F period, significantly ruled by the Snake, a sign which is unfavourable for the Monkey. Elvis, his health failing, fell into decline and in 1977, also a Snake year, he died.

FORTUNE COLUMNS

YEAR	1935	1944	1954	1964	1974
AGE (NATAL MONTH)	9	19	29	39	49
ANIMAL	OX	Tiger	Rabbit	Dragon	Snake	Horse

CODE LETTERS

Ox	Tiger	Rabbit	Dragon	Snake
B	C	D	E	F

SUPPLEMENTARY CHARTS

CHINESE SOLAR AND LUNAR YEARS

YEAR	BEFORE	BEGINNING OF SPRING	AFTER	NEW YEAR FESTIVAL	YEAR	BEFORE	BEGINNING OF SPRING	AFTER	NEW YEAR FESTIVAL
1924	Pig	5 Feb	Rat	5 Feb	1945	Monkey	4 Feb	Rooster	13 Feb
1925	Rat	4 Feb	Ox	24 Jan	1946	Rooster	4 Feb	Dog	2 Feb
1926	Ox	4 Feb	Tiger	13 Feb	1947	Dog	4 Feb	Pig	22 Jan
1927	Tiger	5 Feb	Rabbit	2 Feb	1948	Pig	5 Feb	Rat	10 Feb
1928	Rabbit	5 Feb	Dragon	23 Jan	1949	Rat	4 Feb	Ox	29 Jan
1929	Dragon	4 Feb	Snake	10 Feb	1950	Ox	4 Feb	Tiger	17 Feb
1930	Snake	4 Feb	Horse	30 Jan	1951	Tiger	4 Feb	Rabbit	6 Feb
1931	Horse	5 Feb	Sheep	17 Feb	1952	Rabbit	5 Feb	Dragon	27 Jan
1932	Sheep	5 Feb	Monkey	6 Feb	1953	Dragon	4 Feb	Snake	14 Feb
1933	Monkey	4 Feb	Rooster	26 Jan	1954	Snake	4 Feb	Horse	3 Feb
1934	Rooster	4 Feb	Dog	14 Feb	1955	Horse	4 Feb	Sheep	24 Jan
1935	Dog	5 Feb	Pig	4 Feb	1956	Sheep	5 Feb	Monkey	12 Feb
1936	Pig	5 Feb	Rat	24 Jan	1957	Monkey	4 Feb	Rooster	31 Jan
1937	Rat	4 Feb	Ox	11 Feb	1958	Rooster	4 Feb	Dog	18 Feb
1938	Ox	4 Feb	Tiger	31 Jan	1959	Dog	4 Feb	Pig	8 Feb
1939	Tiger	5 Feb	Rabbit	19 Feb	1960	Pig	5 Feb	Rat	28 Jan
1940	Rabbit	5 Feb	Dragon	8 Feb	1961	Rat	4 Feb	Ox	15 Feb
1941	Dragon	4 Feb	Snake	27 Jan	1962	Ox	4 Feb	Tiger	5 Feb
1942	Snake	4 Feb	Horse	15 Feb	1963	Tiger	4 Feb	Rabbit	25 Jan
1943	Horse	5 Feb	Sheep	5 Feb	1964	Rabbit	5 Feb	Dragon	13 Feb
1944	Sheep	5 Feb	Monkey	25 Jan	1965	Dragon	4 Feb	Snake	2 Feb

SOLAR AND LUNAR YEARS AND MONTHS

The Chinese lunar and solar years are based strictly on astronomical phenomena, so it is not feasible to give dates that will be the same each year. The solar year is closer to the Western year but the starts of the solar months may not be the same each year. Our extra day in leap years, and the tendency of the heavens to slip back one degree every 70 years means that there are some variations in the start of the year and the following months. The lunar year, based on the New Moon, is different every year. The Chinese use the lunar calendar for the start of the New Year celebrations, but the solar calendar for their horoscopes.

YEAR	BEFORE	BEGINNING OF SPRING	AFTER	NEW YEAR FESTIVAL
1966	Snake	4 Feb	Horse	21 Jan
1967	Horse	4 Feb	Sheep	9 Feb
1968	Sheep	5 Feb	Monkey	30 Jan
1969	Monkey	4 Feb	Rooster	17 Feb
1970	Rooster	4 Feb	Dog	6 Feb
1971	Dog	4 Feb	Pig	27 Jan
1972	Pig	5 Feb	Rat	15 Feb
1973	Rat	4 Feb	Ox	3 Feb
1974	Ox	4 Feb	Tiger	23 Jan
1975	Tiger	4 Feb	Rabbit	11 Feb
1976	Rabbit	5 Feb	Dragon	31 Jan
1977	Dragon	4 Feb	Snake	18 Feb
1978	Snake	4 Feb	Horse	7 Feb
1979	Horse	4 Feb	Sheep	28 Jan
1980	Sheep	5 Feb	Monkey	16 Feb
1981	Monkey	4 Feb	Rooster	5 Feb
1982	Rooster	4 Feb	Dog	25 Jan
1983	Dog	4 Feb	Pig	13 Feb
1984	Pig	4 Feb	Rat	2 Feb
1985	Rat	4 Feb	Ox	20 Feb
1986	Ox	4 Feb	Tiger	9 Feb

YEAR	BEFORE	BEGINNING OF SPRING	AFTER	NEW YEAR FESTIVAL
1987	Tiger	4 Feb	Rabbit	29 Jan
1988	Rabbit	4 Feb	Dragon	17 Feb
1989	Dragon	4 Feb	Snake	6 Feb
1990	Snake	4 Feb	Horse	27 Jan
1991	Horse	4 Feb	Sheep	15 Feb
1992	Sheep	4 Feb	Monkey	4 Feb
1993	Monkey	4 Feb	Rooster	23 Jan
1994	Rooster	4 Feb	Dog	10 Feb
1995	Dog	4 Feb	Pig	31 Jan
1996	Pig	4 Feb	Rat	19 Feb
1997	Rat	4 Feb	Ox	7 Feb
1998	Ox	4 Feb	Tiger	28 Jan
1999	Tiger	4 Feb	Rabbit	16 Feb
2000	Rabbit	4 Feb	Dragon	5 Feb
2001	Dragon	4 Feb	Snake	24 Jan
2002	Snake	4 Feb	Horse	12 Feb
2003	Horse	4 Feb	Sheep	1 Feb
2004	Sheep	4 Feb	Monkey	22 Jan
2005	Monkey	4 Feb	Rooster	9 Feb
2006	Rooster	4 Feb	Dog	29 Jan
2007	Dog	4 Feb	Pig	18 Feb

DATES OF THE SOLAR MONTHS

	OX	TIGER	RABBIT	DRAGON	SNAKE	HORSE	SHEEP	MONKEY	ROOSTER	DOG	PIG	RAT
1924	6.1	5.2	6.3	5.4	6.5	6.6	8.7	8.8	8.9	8.10	8.11	7.12
1925	6.1	4.2	6.3	5.4	6.5	6.6	7.7	8.8	8.9	9.10	8.11	8.12
1926	6.1	4.2	6.3	5.4	6.5	6.6	8.7	8.8	8.9	9.10	8.11	8.12
1927	6.1	5.2	6.3	6.4	6.5	7.6	8.7	8.8	8.9	9.10	8.11	7.12
1928	6.1	5.2	6.3	5.4	6.5	6.6	7.7	8.8	8.9	8.10	7.11	7.12
1929	6.1	4.2	6.3	5.4	6.5	6.6	7.7	8.8	8.9	9.10	8.11	8.12
1930	6.1	4.2	6.3	5.4	6.5	6.6	8.7	8.8	8.9	9.10	8.11	8.12
1931	6.1	5.2	6.3	6.4	6.5	7.6	8.7	8.8	8.9	9.10	8.11	7.12
1932	6.1	5.2	6.3	5.4	6.5	6.6	7.7	8.8	8.9	8.10	7.11	7.12
1933	6.1	4.2	6.3	5.4	6.5	6.6	7.7	8.8	8.9	9.10	8.11	8.12
1934	6.1	4.2	6.3	5.4	6.5	6.6	8.7	8.8	8.9	9.10	8.11	8.12
1935	6.1	5.2	6.3	6.4	6.5	6.6	8.7	8.8	8.9	9.10	8.11	7.12
1936	6.1	5.2	6.3	5.4	6.5	6.6	7.7	8.8	8.9	8.10	7.11	7.12
1937	6.1	4.2	6.3	5.4	6.5	6.6	7.7	8.8	8.9	9.10	8.11	8.12
1938	6.1	4.2	6.3	5.4	6.5	6.6	8.7	8.8	8.9	9.10	8.11	8.12
1939	6.1	5.2	6.3	6.4	6.5	6.6	8.7	8.8	8.9	9.10	8.11	7.12
1940	6.1	5.2	6.3	5.4	6.5	6.6	7.7	8.8	8.9	8.10	7.11	7.12
1941	6.1	4.2	6.3	5.4	6.5	6.6	7.7	8.8	8.9	9.10	8.11	8.12
1942	6.1	4.2	6.3	5.4	6.5	6.6	8.7	8.8	8.9	9.10	8.11	8.12
1943	6.1	5.2	6.3	6.4	6.5	6.6	8.7	8.8	8.9	9.10	8.11	7.12
1944	6.1	5.2	6.3	5.4	5.5	6.6	7.7	8.8	8.9	8.10	7.11	7.12
1945	6.1	4.2	6.3	5.4	6.5	6.6	7.7	8.8	8.9	8.10	8.11	8.12
1946	6.1	4.2	6.3	5.4	6.5	6.6	8.7	8.8	8.9	9.10	8.11	8.12
1947	6.1	4.2	6.3	5.4	6.5	6.6	8.7	8.8	8.9	9.10	8.11	8.12
1948	6.1	5.2	5.3	5.4	5.5	6.6	7.7	7.8	8.9	8.10	7.11	7.12
1949	5.1	4.2	6.3	5.4	6.5	6.6	7.7	8.8	8.9	8.10	8.11	7.12
1950	6.1	4.2	6.3	5.4	6.5	6.6	8.7	8.8	8.9	9.10	8.11	8.12
1951	6.1	4.2	6.3	5.4	6.5	6.6	8.7	8.8	8.9	9.10	8.11	7.12
1952	6.1	5.2	5.3	5.4	5.5	6.6	7.7	7.8	8.9	8.10	7.11	7.12
1953	5.1	4.2	6.3	5.4	6.5	6.6	7.7	8.8	8.9	8.10	8.11	7.12
1954	6.1	4.2	6.3	5.4	6.5	6.6	8.7	8.8	8.9	9.10	8.11	8.12
1955	6.1	4.2	6.3	5.4	6.5	6.6	8.7	8.8	8.9	9.10	8.11	7.12
1956	6.1	5.2	5.3	5.4	5.5	6.6	7.7	7.8	8.9	8.10	7.11	7.12
1957	5.1	4.2	6.3	5.4	6.5	6.6	7.7	8.8	8.9	8.10	8.11	7.12
1958	6.1	4.2	6.3	5.4	6.5	6.6	7.7	8.8	8.9	9.10	8.11	8.12
1959	6.1	4.2	6.3	5.4	6.5	6.6	8.7	8.8	8.9	9.10	8.11	7.12
1960	6.1	5.2	5.3	5.4	5.5	6.6	7.7	7.8	7.9	8.10	7.11	7.12
1961	5.1	4.2	6.3	5.4	6.5	6.6	7.7	8.8	8.9	8.10	7.11	7.12
1962	6.1	4.2	6.3	5.4	6.5	6.6	7.7	8.8	8.9	9.10	8.11	8.12
1963	6.1	4.2	6.3	5.4	6.5	6.6	8.7	8.8	8.9	9.10	8.11	7.12
1964	6.1	5.2	5.3	5.4	5.5	6.6	7.7	7.8	7.9	8.10	7.11	7.12
1965	5.1	4.2	6.3	5.4	6.5	6.6	7.7	8.8	8.9	8.10	7.11	7.12
1966	6.1	4.2	6.3	5.4	6.5	6.6	7.7	8.8	8.9	9.10	8.11	8.12
1967	6.1	4.2	6.3	5.4	6.5	6.6	8.7	8.8	8.9	9.10	8.11	7.12

	OX	TIGER	RABBIT	DRAGON	SNAKE	HORSE	SHEEP	MONKEY	ROOSTER	DOG	PIG	RAT
1968	6.1	5.2	5.3	5.4	5.5	5.6	7.7	7.8	7.9	8.10	7.11	7.12
1969	5.1	4.2	6.3	5.4	6.5	6.6	7.7	8.8	8.9	8.10	7.11	7.12
1970	6.1	4.2	6.3	5.4	6.5	6.6	7.7	8.8	8.9	9.10	8.11	8.12
1971	6.1	4.2	6.3	5.4	6.5	6.6	8.7	8.8	8.9	9.10	8.11	7.12
1972	6.1	5.2	5.3	5.4	5.5	5.6	7.7	7.8	7.9	8.10	7.11	7.12
1973	5.1	4.2	6.3	5.4	5.5	6.6	7.7	8.8	8.9	8.10	7.11	7.12
1974	6.1	4.2	6.3	5.4	6.5	6.6	7.7	8.8	8.9	9.10	8.11	8.12
1975	6.1	4.2	6.3	5.4	6.5	6.6	8.7	8.8	8.9	9.10	8.11	7.12
1976	6.1	5.2	5.3	4.4	5.5	5.6	7.7	7.8	7.9	8.10	7.11	7.12
1977	5.1	4.2	6.3	5.4	5.5	6.6	7.7	7.8	8.9	8.10	7.11	7.12
1978	6.1	4.2	6.3	5.4	6.5	6.6	7.7	8.8	8.9	8.10	8.11	8.12
1979	6.1	4.2	6.3	5.4	6.5	6.6	8.7	8.8	8.9	9.10	8.11	7.12
1980	6.1	5.2	5.3	4.4	5.5	5.6	7.7	7.8	7.9	8.10	7.11	7.12
1981	5.1	4.2	6.3	5.4	5.5	6.6	7.7	7.8	8.9	8.10	7.11	7.12
1982	6.1	4.2	6.3	5.4	6.5	6.6	7.7	8.8	8.9	8.10	8.11	8.12
1983	6.1	4.2	6.3	5.4	6.5	6.6	8.7	8.8	8.9	9.10	8.11	7.12
1984	6.1	4.2	5.3	4.4	5.5	5.6	7.7	7.8	7.9	8.10	7.11	7.12
1985	5.1	4.2	5.3	5.4	5.5	6.6	7.7	7.8	8.9	8.10	7.11	7.12
1986	5.1	4.2	6.3	5.4	6.5	6.6	7.7	8.8	8.9	8.10	8.11	7.12
1987	6.1	4.2	6.3	5.4	6.5	6.6	7.7	8.8	8.9	9.10	8.11	7.12
1988	6.1	4.2	5.3	4.4	5.5	5.6	7.7	7.8	7.9	8.10	7.11	7.12
1989	5.1	4.2	5.3	5.4	5.5	6.6	7.7	7.8	7.9	8.10	7.11	7.12
1990	5.1	4.2	6.3	5.4	6.5	6.6	7.7	8.8	8.9	8.10	8.11	7.12
1991	6.1	4.2	6.3	5.4	6.5	6.6	7.7	8.8	8.9	9.10	8.11	7.12
1992	6.1	4.2	5.3	4.4	5.5	5.6	7.7	7.8	7.9	8.10	7.11	7.12
1993	5.1	4.2	5.3	5.4	5.5	6.6	7.7	7.8	7.9	8.10	7.11	7.12
1994	5.1	4.2	6.3	5.4	6.5	6.6	7.7	8.8	8.9	8.10	7.11	7.12
1995	6.1	4.2	6.3	5.4	6.5	6.6	7.7	8.8	8.9	9.10	8.11	7.12
1996	6.1	4.2	5.3	4.4	5.5	5.6	7.7	7.8	7.9	8.10	7.11	7.12
1997	5.1	4.2	5.3	5.4	5.5	5.6	7.7	7.8	7.9	8.10	7.11	7.12
1998	5.1	4.2	6.3	5.4	6.5	6.6	7.7	8.8	8.9	8.10	8.11	7.12
1999	6.1	4.2	6.3	5.4	6.5	6.6	7.7	8.8	8.9	9.10	7.11	7.12
2000	6.1	4.2	5.3	4.4	5.5	5.6	7.7	7.8	7.9	8.10	7.11	7.12
2001	5.1	4.2	5.3	5.4	5.5	5.6	7.7	7.8	7.9	8.10	7.11	7.12
2002	5.1	4.2	6.3	5.4	6.5	6.6	7.7	8.8	8.9	8.10	8.11	7.12
2003	6.1	4.2	6.3	5.4	6.5	6.6	7.7	8.8	8.9	9.10	8.11	7.12
2004	6.1	4.2	5.3	4.4	5.5	5.6	7.7	7.8	7.9	8.10	7.11	7.12
2005	6.1	4.2	5.3	5.4	5.5	5.6	7.7	7.8	7.9	8.10	7.11	7.12
2006	6.1	4.2	6.3	5.4	6.5	6.6	7.7	8.8	8.9	8.10	8.11	7.12
2007	6.1	4.2	6.3	5.4	6.5	6.6	7.7	8.8	8.9	9.10	8.11	7.12
2008	6.1	4.2	5.3	4.4	5.5	5.6	7.7	7.8	7.9	8.10	7.11	7.12
2009	5.1	4.2	5.3	5.4	5.5	5.6	7.7	7.8	7.9	8.10	7.11	7.12
2010	5.1	4.2	6.3	5.4	5.5	6.6	7.7	7.8	8.9	8.10	7.11	7.12

INDEX

ACKNOWLEDGEMENTS

AUTHOR ACKNOWLEDGEMENTS

I would like to acknowledge the kindness of Professor Xu Zhentao, Purple Mountain Observatory, Nanjing; the most Rev. Xu Jing-Ding, and Chen He Dan, of the World Yi Jing Conference, Taipei. And special thanks to Phap Rop Miao, Birmingham, and the attentive staff at my second home, the Globe Ground Lounge, Manchester Airport.

PUBLISHER'S ACKNOWLEDGEMENTS

Executive Editor: David Alexander
Managing Editor: Clare Churly
Production Manager: Louise Hall

Designed and produced for Hamlyn by
The Bridgewater Book Company

Creative Director: Terry Jeavons
Editorial Director: Jason Hook
Designer: Alison Hughes
Editor: Fiona Biggs
Page makeup: Chris & Jane Lanaway

Illustrators: Rhian Nest James, Pauline Allen, Sarah Young

Bridgewater Books would like to thank the following for the permission to reproduce copyright material: Corbis Stock Market page 135.